SIMPLE GRACES

Charming Quilts and Companion Projects

KIM DIEHL

Martingale®
& COMPANY

Simple Graces:
Charming Quilts and Companion Projects
© 2010 by Kim Diehl

That Patchwork Place® is an imprint of
Martingale & Company®.

Martingale & Company
19021 120th Ave. NE, Suite 102
Bothell, WA 98011 USA
www.martingale-pub.com

Printed in China
15 14 13 12 11   8 7 6 5 4

Library of Congress Cataloging-in-
Publication Data is available upon request.

ISBN: 978-1-56477-992-2

Credits

President & CEO: Tom Wierzbicki
Editor in Chief: Mary V. Green
Managing Editor: Tina Cook
Developmental Editor: Karen Costello Soltys
Design Director: Stan Green
Technical Editor: Laurie Baker
Copy Editor: Sheila Chapman Ryan
Production Manager: Regina Girard
Illustrator: Laurel Strand
Cover & Text Designer: Stan Green
Photographer: Brent Kane

Mission Statement

Dedicated to providing quality products and
service to inspire creativity.

DEDICATION

To my special girls, Katie Pie and Molly Dolly, for loving your mom so much.

ACKNOWLEDGMENTS

To Heather Lofstrom, Vicki Jones, and Jan Watkins, thank you for so generously devoting your time and incredible patchwork skills to stitching two of the quilts (and several hundred yo-yos) for this book. And to Deb Behrend, you have my complete appreciation for your impeccable workmanship and wonderful way with color.

To Celeste Freiberg and especially Deborah Poole, your machine quilting is almost too exquisite for words and elevates my quilts well beyond what I could achieve on my own, so I will simply say a heartfelt "thank-you."

To Lianne Anderson, your beautiful home was like the cherry on top of the sundae as we photographed the quilts and projects for this book—I appreciate your hospitality and generosity!

I'd like to give my sincere thanks to everyone at Martingale & Company who had a hand in helping me shape my ideas for this book, especially to Stan Green and Brent Kane for your incomparable expertise during the photo shoot. To Laurie Baker, you continue to make me look like one smart cookie while also managing to be a complete joy to work with—what an awesome combination.

To Janome America, many thanks for the pure joy of stitching my quilts and projects on your Memory Craft 11000 sewing machine.

To Fairfield Processing Corporation, thank you for your Soft Touch batting, which always gives my finished quilts such a warm and inviting feel.

And last, a big thank-you to Jo Morton, as well as Pam Soliday and Janet Nesbitt of the Buggy Barn, for your beautiful fabrics which blended so perfectly with my own fabric designs and stash to help create the scrap-basket look I love in my quilts.

CONTENTS

INTRODUCTION

Have you ever noticed the truly endless creative possibilities that each quilt brings? When I begin mulling over ideas for a new project, settling upon just one finished look or style when there are potentially so many different design paths I could explore is sometimes the very hardest choice of all.

 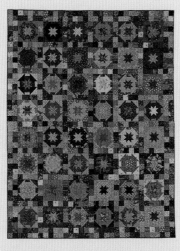 

We can be faced with a thousand and one different design decisions while planning any given quilt, and changing just one tiny element can completely transform the outcome and send the quilt in a whole new direction. And because so many quilts hold the promise of becoming so many different things, why should any of us have to settle upon just one?

As I prepare and stitch each new quilt, there are often several little ideas taking shape and percolating in the back of my mind for additional projects. For instance, isolating just one single aspect of my original design might result in the perfect starting point for a second quilt. But why stop there? Adding an embellishment to the second project and making a few simple color adjustments could easily result in an entirely different third project . . . and notice that I said "project," not "quilt"! Where is it written that a quilt design can only be used to make a quilt?

Always have fun with your quiltmaking and search for unique ways to apply the designs to everyday items. Looking beyond the pattern presentation of your quilts can help unlock their hidden potential and really liberate your creative instincts. You'll find that even small changes can produce surprisingly big results, and what better way to express your own personal flair? Simply reversing a traditional color scheme and stitching your block design or appliqués from neutral tones onto a dark background can result in a dramatic and unexpected look. Or think about adding dimensional embellishments such as buttons or yo-yos to basic patchwork designs for a hint of the unexpected. Finally, try using wool in combination with your favorite quilting fabrics for a charming blend of texture and print, or even consider substituting it entirely. You may find yourself having so much fun being adventurous and making up your own rules that you'll decide doing what's expected is highly overrated.

Here's hoping that these projects will spark some fresh and innovative ideas of your own—once you've embraced the creativity that you alone can bring to your quiltmaking, you may discover that your hardest choice of all will be deciding when to quit!

QUILTMAKING PRINCIPLES

The information in this section provides the techniques and procedures used to piece and assemble the projects included in this book. Some of these methods are commonly practiced while others were developed on my own as I learned the techniques used in quiltmaking.

Yardage Requirements

The project instructions in this book assume a 42" useable width of fabric after prewashing and removing selvages. To make the best use of your yardage, always cut your pieces in the order given.

Rotary Cutting

Unless otherwise noted, please cut all pieces on the straight of grain and across the width of the fabric. To speed the cutting process, I routinely fold my pressed fabric in half with the selvages together, and then in half once more. This method results in four pieces with each cut. Of course, the size of the pieces will determine how many folds you can make.

Place the folded fabric on your cutting mat, aligning the folded edge with a horizontal line on the marked grid. Position your ruler on top of the fabric and make a vertical cut along one side to establish a straight edge. Measure and cut your pieces from this edge.

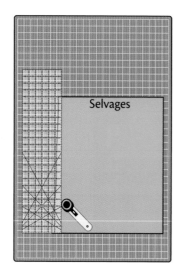

To cut half-square triangles from a square (or layered stack of squares), lay your ruler diagonally across the square, with the cutting edge directly over the corners, and make the cut.

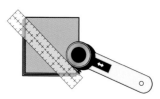

Cutting Bias Strips

For projects that utilize bias strips (lengths of cloth that have been cut diagonally rather than across the width of fabric), I suggest the following cutting method. I love this method of cutting bias strips because it enables me to work with a manageable size of cloth, while producing strips that are approximately twice the cut length once they're unfolded.

1. After pressing the fabric to remove any wrinkles or folds, lay it in a single layer on a large cutting mat. Grasp one corner of the fabric and fold it back to form a layered triangle in any size of your choosing, aligning the top straight edge with the straight grain of the bottom layer of fabric.

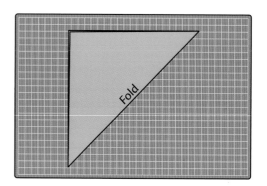

2. Rotate the layered piece of cloth, aligning the folded edge with a cutting line on your mat (I've found that resting an acrylic ruler over the fabric fold to align it will help define this edge and ensure it is positioned in a straight line, eliminating the chance of a "dog-leg" curve in your strips).

3. Use an acrylic ruler and rotary cutter to cut through the folded edge of cloth 2" to 3" away from the pointed end. With the ruler lined up with the lines on the mat, begin cutting your strips at measured intervals from this edge as designated by the pattern instructions.

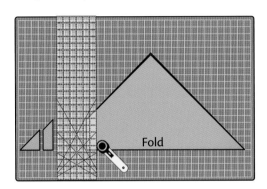
Fold

4. Square off the strip ends, trimming them to the desired length, or join multiple lengths together end to end to achieve the necessary length; press the seams allowances to one side, all in the same direction. Experience has taught me that if your strips will be used for bias tube stems, using straight, *not* diagonal, seams to join multiple lengths will provide the best results, because bias bars tend to catch on diagonal seams.

Trim ends.

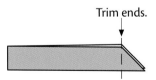

Pinning

I recommend pinning your layered patchwork pieces together at regular intervals, including all sewn seams and intersections. A good tip for achieving a consistently sewn seam that extends to the back edge of your patchwork is to pin the pieces with glass-head pins. The pin heads can be used to steer the patchwork through the machine in a straight line, eliminating inaccurate seams at the tail end where fishtailing often occurs.

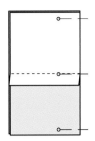

Machine Piecing

Unless otherwise instructed, always join your fabrics with right sides together using a ¼" seam allowance. To achieve an accurate seam allowance, I suggest using a ¼" presser foot made specifically for quiltmaking. You can also easily make a guide using masking tape. To do this, gently lower your sewing-machine needle until the point rests upon the ¼" line of an acrylic ruler. After ensuring that the ruler is resting in a straight position, apply a line of ¼" masking tape to the sewing-machine surface exactly along the ruler's edge, taking care not to cover the feed dogs. Align the edge of the fabrics with this taped line as you feed the pieces through the machine.

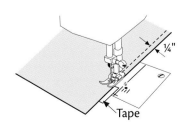
¼"
Tape

Your machine's standard stitch length is perfectly acceptable for patchwork seams, but I routinely shorten my stitch length slightly to achieve finished seams that are sturdy and invisible, particularly for smaller-scale projects.

Chain Piecing

For projects with many pieces to be joined, chain piecing will save both time and thread. To chain piece, simply feed your patchwork units through the sewing machine one after another without snipping the threads between each. When you finish sewing the units, cut the threads connecting them and press as instructed.

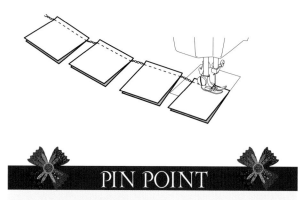

Pressing Seams

Pressing well is crucial for patchwork that fits together properly. I recommend using a hot, dry iron and the following steps when pressing your seams.

1. Place the patchwork on a firm-surfaced ironing board, with the fabric you wish to press toward (usually the darker hue) on top. On the wrong side of the fabric, briefly bring your iron down onto the sewn seam to warm the fabric.
2. Lift the iron and fold the top piece of fabric back to expose the right sides of the fabrics. While the fabric is still warm, run your

fingernail along the sewn thread line to relax the fibers at the fold. Press the seam flat from the right side of the patchwork. The seam allowance will now lie under the fabric that was originally positioned on top.

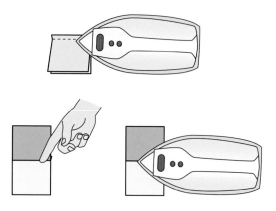

I suggest pressing without steam because this will enable you to easily modify your seams if adjustments to your patchwork become necessary.

Pressing Triangle Units

Several projects in this book call for stitch-and-fold triangle units that are created by layering a square with a drawn diagonal line on top of a second square or rectangle. After stitching the pair together on the line, I recommend the following steps.

1. Fold the top triangle back and align its corner with the corner of the bottom piece of fabric to keep it square; press in place.
2. Trim away the excess layers of fabric beneath the top triangle, leaving a ¼" seam allowance.

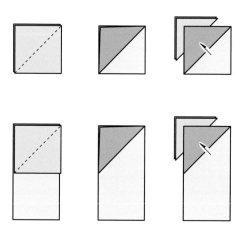

The seam allowances of triangle units are commonly trimmed *before* they are pressed, but I've found that this pressing method produces accurate patchwork that seldom requires squaring up.

PIN POINT

Compensating for Triangle Seam Allowances

Before stitching any layered pair together along the drawn diagonal line, I routinely determine which corner of the unit I'll be pressing the top triangle of fabric toward. Stitching about a thread's width closer to this corner immediately *next* to the drawn line helps to compensate for the fabric that is lost to the seam allowance fold once the unit has been pressed.

Appliqué Methods

Different methods of appliqué can be appropriate for different quilts, depending upon the quilt's intended use and the amount of time you wish to dedicate to making it. You'll find my techniques for three different styles of appliqué in this section, making it easy to personalize the finished look of your projects, the degree of skill required, and the amount of time devoted to stitching them.

Invisible Machine Appliqué

In addition to your standard quiltmaking supplies, the following tools and products are needed for this method:

- .004 monofilament thread in smoke and clear colors
- Awl or stiletto tool with a sharp point
- Bias bars of various widths
- Embroidery scissors with a fine, sharp point
- Freezer paper
- Iron with a sharp pressing point (travel-sized or mini appliqué irons work well for this technique)
- Liquid fabric basting glue, water soluble and acid free (my favorite brand is Quilter's Choice Basting Glue by Beacon Adhesives)

- Open-toe presser foot
- Pressing board with a firm surface
- Sewing machine with adjustable tension control, capable of producing a tiny zigzag stitch
- Size 75/11 (or smaller) machine-quilting needles
- Tweezers with rounded tips

Choosing Your Monofilament Thread

There are currently two types of monofilament thread (sometimes called "invisible thread") available that work well for invisible machine appliqué: nylon and polyester. Both types have their own characteristics and strengths and can bring different benefits to your appliqué projects.

In my experience, nylon thread tends to produce results that are slightly more invisible, but extra care should be used as your project is being assembled and pressed because this thread can be weakened by the heat of a very hot iron. For best results when working with nylon thread, avoid applying prolonged or high heat directly to the front of your appliqués and press any nearby seams carefully. Once the project is finished and bound, I've found that the stitched appliqués will stand up well to everyday use and care. When I use nylon monofilament for my own projects, I've had very good results using the YLI brand.

If you'd like an extra measure of confidence that your appliqués will remain securely in place, even if they're inadvertently pressed from the front and exposed to direct heat from your iron, you may wish to use polyester monofilament thread. I find that the look of polyester monofilament can vary greatly from one brand to another, with some appearing thicker or even shinier than others. Depending upon the brand you choose, the monofilament may be slightly more visible on your stitched appliqués. For projects where I've opted to use a polyester product I've been very pleased with the Sulky brand, because I feel the results most closely resemble those that are achieved when using nylon.

Ultimately, I recommend that you experiment with both types of monofilament and make this decision based upon your own personal results and preferences.

Preparing Pattern Templates

For projects featuring multiple appliqués made from one pattern, I've found that being able to trace around a sturdy template to make the required number of pattern pieces, rather than tracing over the pattern sheet numerous times, speeds the process tremendously and gives consistent results. Keep in mind as you make your templates that any shape can be modified to fit your skill level—points with thin tips can be fattened and narrow inner curves can be plumped. Your resulting appliqués will look essentially the same, but your shapes will be much easier to work with. To make a sturdy paper template for tracing pattern pieces, follow these steps.

1. Cut a piece of freezer paper about twice as large as your shape. Use a pencil to trace the pattern onto one end of the non-waxy side of the paper. Fold the freezer paper in half, waxy sides together, and use a hot, dry iron to fuse the folded paper layers together.
2. Cut out the shape exactly on the drawn line, taking care to duplicate it accurately.

Preparing Paper Pattern Pieces

Pattern pieces are used differently than pattern templates; templates are simply a tool used to easily trace your shapes, while individual paper pattern pieces are what you will use as you prepare your appliqués from cloth. Always cut paper pattern pieces on the drawn lines; you'll add the seam allowances later as you cut your shapes from fabric. To achieve smooth pattern edges, I suggest moving the paper, rather than the scissors, as you take long cutting strokes.

Use the prepared template (or pattern sheet, if you are preparing fewer than a dozen pieces) to trace the specified number of pattern pieces onto the non-waxy side of a piece of freezer paper. To save time when many pieces are required, stack the freezer paper up to six layers deep (with the waxy sides facing down), anchor them together, and cut several shapes at once. To easily anchor the paper layers you can pin them through the center of your shapes, but I've found that a quick and simple method is to use a stapler to staple them together at regular intervals about ¼" *outside* the shape,

cut out the pattern pieces, and then discard the remaining stapled background areas.

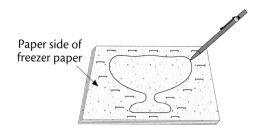

Paper side of freezer paper

Mirror-image pieces can easily be prepared by tracing the pattern onto the non-waxy side of one end of a strip of freezer paper, and then folding it accordion style in widths to fit your shape. Anchor the layers together as described above and cut out the shape. When you separate the pieces, every other shape will be a mirror image.

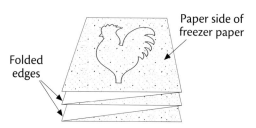

Paper side of freezer paper

Folded edges

I consistently use the accordion-fold technique for quickly making multiple pattern pieces of any shape that does not have an obvious direction (such as a leaf), because this method speeds the process and adds interest to my finished quilts.

Preparing Appliqués

1. Apply a small amount of glue from a fabric glue stick to the *non-waxy* side of each pattern piece and affix it to the wrong side of your fabric, leaving approximately ½" between each shape for seam allowances. Experience has taught me that positioning the longest lines or curves of each shape on the diagonal is best, because bias edges are easier to manipulate than straight-grain edges when pressing the seam allowances over onto the paper pattern pieces.

Waxy side of freezer paper up

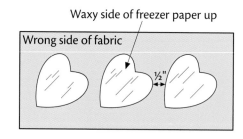

Wrong side of fabric
½"

2. Using embroidery scissors, cut out each shape, adding a scant ¼" seam allowance around the paper.

I've discovered that it's easier to press and prepare the seam allowances of all outer curves and points without clipping them, but the seam allowances of inner points or pronounced inner curves should be clipped once at the center point, taking care not to clip into the paper. If you're not sure whether an inner seam allowance curve requires a clip, try pressing it without one—if the fabric follows the shape of the curve easily, you've eliminated a step!

Clip inner points
to paper edge.

PIN POINT

Extending the Life of Your Ironing Board

To easily protect your ironing board surface and keep it in "like-new" condition for longer, try ironing a sheet of freezer paper onto the cloth pad before you begin pressing your appliqués. The paper will protect the surface from any fabric adhesives, and once your pressing is complete it can be peeled away and discarded.

Pressing Appliqués

Well-pressed shapes will help produce finished appliqués with flawless curves that appear hand stitched.

I suggest using the steps that follow to press the seam allowance of each appliqué, keeping the edge you are working with furthest from you at approximately the twelve o'clock to one o'clock position. As you follow these pressing steps, keep in mind that if you're right-handed, you'll want to work around the shape from right to left as you press, rotating the appliqué clockwise in small increments to keep the area you are pressing

at approximately the top of the shape. If you're left-handed, simply reverse the direction to press and rotate the appliqué. Pressing in the suggested direction is important, because it will direct the seam allowance of your pressed points toward your "smart" hand, enabling you to easily use your awl to finish them with crisp, sharp results.

1. Beginning at a straight or gently curved edge and working your way around the entire shape, use the pad of your finger to smooth the fabric seam allowance over onto the paper pattern piece, following with the point of a hot, dry iron to firmly press it in place. To avoid puckered appliqué edges, always draw the seam allowance slightly back toward the last section pressed. I routinely let the point of my iron rest on each newly pressed section of seam allowance as I draw the next section over onto the paper pattern piece, because this lengthens the amount of time the fabric receives heat from the iron and helps to fuse it more firmly to the paper.

Direct seam allowance
toward center of shape.

2. For sharp outer points, press the seam allowance so the folded edge of the fabric extends beyond the first side of the pattern point, snugging the fabric firmly up against the paper edge. Fold over the seam allowance on the remaining side of the point and continue pressing. After the seam allowance of the entire piece has been pressed, apply a small amount of glue stick to the bottom of the folded flap of fabric at the point. If the seam-allowance flap will be visible from the front of the appliqué, use the point of an awl or stiletto to drag the fabric in and away from the appliqué edge (not

Flawless Appliqué Curves and Circles

Take care to keep your seam allowances for pronounced curves and small circles to a scant ¼", and sometimes even as narrow as ⅛" for very small curved areas, because this will enable the fabric to easily conform to your shape as you press and prepare your seam allowances. If you find that your pressed circles are looking more like stop signs than berries, try working in smaller increments as you draw each section of fabric seam allowance over onto the freezer-paper pattern pieces, because this will help the fabric to smoothly hug the curves of the paper.

down from the point, as this will blunt it), and touch it with the point of a hot iron to heat set the glue and fuse it in place.

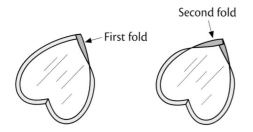

Second fold

First fold

3. To prepare an inner point or pronounced inner curve, stop pressing the seam allowance just shy of the center clipped section. Reaching under the appliqué at the clip, use the pad of your finger to smooth the clipped section of fabric snugly onto the paper, following immediately behind with the iron in a sweeping motion to fuse the fibers in place onto the paper.

Always turn your prepared appliqué over to the front to evaluate your pressing and adjust any areas that could be improved. Tiny imperfections can be smoothed by nudging them with the point of your hot iron, and more pronounced imperfections can be loosened and re-pressed from the back.

Making Bias-Tube Stems and Vines

To achieve finished stems and vines that can be curved flawlessly and don't require the seam allowances to be turned under, I use bias tubes. After cutting the strips specified in the project instructions (refer to "Cutting Bias Strips" on page 8 for guidelines), prepare them as follows:

1. With *wrong* sides together, fold the strip in half lengthwise and stitch a scant ¼" from the long raw edges to form a tube. For any stem sewn from a strip 1" or less in width, you may need to trim the seam allowance to approximately ⅛" so that it will be hidden when the stem is viewed from the front.

Scant ¼" seam allowance

Trim seam allowance to ⅛" for narrow stems.

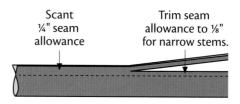

2. Because of seam allowance differences that can occur, the best bias bar width for each project can vary from person to person, even for stems of the same size. Ultimately, I've found it's best to simply choose a bar that will fit comfortably into the sewn tube, and then slide it along as you press the stem flat to one side, centering the seam allowance so it won't be visible from the front.

Bias bar

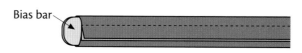

3. Remove the bias bar and place small dots of liquid basting glue at approximately 1" intervals along the seam line underneath the layers of the pressed seam allowance; use a hot, dry iron on the wrong side of the stem to heat set the glue and fuse the seam allowance in place.

Basting Appliqués

Invisible machine appliqué, like hand appliqué, is sewn in layers from the bottom to the top. Keep in mind as you lay out and baste your appliqués that it's a good practice to leave approximately ½" between the outermost appliqués of your design and the raw edge of your background because this will preserve an intact margin of space around each piece after the quilt top has been assembled.

1. Lay out the prepared appliqués on the background to ensure that everything fits and is to your liking. As you lay out your pieces, remember that any appliqué with a raw edge that will be overlapped by another piece (such as a stem) should be overlapped by approximately ¼" to prevent fraying.

2. Remove all but the bottom appliqués and baste them in place. Liquid basting glue is my preferred method because there are no pins to stitch around or remove and the appliqués will not shift or result in shrinkage to the background cloth as they are stitched. I suggest glue basting your appliqués as follows:

Without shifting the appliqué from its position, fold over one half of the shape to expose the back and place small dots of liquid basting glue along the fabric seam allowance at approximately ½" to 1" intervals. Firmly press the glue-basted portion of the appliqué in place and repeat with the remaining half of the shape. From the back, use a hot, dry iron to heat set the glue.

Preparing Your Sewing Machine

Monofilament thread produces results that are nearly invisible and it's easy to use once you know how to prepare your sewing machine. Be sure to match your monofilament color to your appliqué, not your background, choosing a smoke color for medium and dark prints and clear for bright colors and pastels. If you're not sure which color is best, lay a strand of each over your print to audition them. Whenever possible, use the upright spool pin position on your machine for monofilament to facilitate even feed.

1. Use a size 75/11 (or smaller) quilting needle in your sewing machine and thread it with monofilament.

PIN POINT

Irons De-Mystified

On average, a full-sized iron can use up to 1600 watts of power, with travel-sized irons using approximately 800 to 1000 watts, and small irons (such as Clover's mini-iron for appliqué) using less than 100 watts. If you choose one of the smaller low-wattage irons for your appliqué preparation, try using a sawing motion along the fabric seam allowances as you press them, because this will apply additional heat to the cloth to better fuse it in place. For classes, I always recommend leaving your full-sized iron at home and substituting a travel-sized or smaller iron; they work equally well and are more fuse-box friendly when many irons are in use.

2. Wind the bobbin with all-purpose, neutral-colored thread; in my experience, a 50-weight thread works well for this technique in most sewing machines.
NOTE: If your machine's bobbin case features a special eye for use with embroidery techniques, threading your bobbin thread through this opening will often provide additional tension control to perfectly regulate your stitches.

3. Program your sewing machine to the zigzag stitch, adjust the width and length to achieve a tiny stitch as shown below (keeping in mind that your inner stitches should land two or three stitches inside your appliqué, with your outer stitches piercing the background immediately next to the appliqué) and reduce the tension setting. For many sewing machines, a width, length, and tension setting of 1 produces the perfect stitch.

〜〜〜〜〜〜〜〜〜〜〜

Approximate stitch size

Stitching the Appliqués

Before stitching your first invisible-machine-appliqué project, I recommend experimenting with a simple pattern shape to become comfortable with this technique and find the best settings for

Pros and Cons of Pre-Wound Bobbins

While pre-wound bobbins are a wonderful convenience, they can sometimes make it difficult to achieve the perfectly balanced tension needed for invisible machine appliqué. If you are using this type of bobbin and experience tension control issues with your sewing machine during the machine appliqué process, try winding and substituting a bobbin of your own.

your sewing machine. Keep your test piece as a quick reference for future projects, making a note directly on the background fabric as to your machine's width, length, and tension settings, and even whether your machine begins zigzag stitching on the left or the right.

1. Slide the basted appliqué under the sewing-machine needle from front to back to direct the threads behind the machine, positioning a straight or gently curved edge under the needle.

2. Place your fingertip over the monofilament tail or grasp the threads as your machine takes two or three stitches. Lift your finger and continue zigzag stitching around your shape, with your inner stitches landing on the appliqué and your outer stitches piercing the background immediately next to the appliqué. Watch the outer stitches while you sew to keep your appliqué positioned correctly and the inner stitches will naturally fall into place. After a short distance, pause and carefully clip the monofilament tail close to the background.

To maintain good control, stitch each appliqué at a slow to moderate speed, stopping and pivoting as often as needed to keep the edge of your shape

feeding straight toward the needle. Whenever possible, pivot with the needle down inside the appliqué, because the paper pattern piece will stabilize the shape and prevent it from stretching.

- If dots of bobbin thread appear along the front edge of your appliqué as you stitch, further adjust the tension settings on your machine (usually lower) until they disappear.
- If the monofilament thread is visible underneath your appliqué from the back, or the stitches appear loose or loopy, adjust the tension settings (usually higher) until they are secure.

Evaluating Your Stitch Placement

To evaluate your zigzag stitches and ensure that they are catching all of your appliqué edges, hold a completed appliqué piece up to the light and view it with the light shining from behind. Doing this will highlight the tiny holes left by the needle, and you can immediately tell where each of your stitches are landing to make any necessary adjustments for future pieces.

3. To firmly secure an inner point, stitch to the position where the inner stitch rests exactly on the inner point of the appliqué and stop. Pivot the fabric, and with the appliqué inner point at a right angle to the needle, continue stitching. For pieces with inner points that seem delicate, I often pivot and stitch this area twice to secure it well.

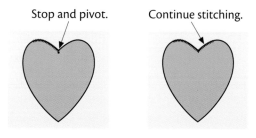

Stop and pivot. Continue stitching.

4. To secure an outer point, stitch to the position where the outer stitch lands exactly next to the appliqué point in the background and stop. Pivot the fabric and continue stitching along

the next side of the shape. As you begin sewing again, a second stitch will drop into the point of the appliqué.

Stop and pivot.   Continue stitching.

5. Continue stitching around the edge of the appliqué until you overlap your starting point by approximately ¼". End with a locking stitch if your sewing machine offers this feature (either on the appliqué or on the background, wherever it will best be hidden), or, for machines without this feature, extend the overlapped area to about ½" to secure the appliqué well.

PIN POINT

Locking Stitches

Using a locking stitch to complete each appliqué provides a benefit above and beyond the security of your finished piece. When you use a locking stitch it communicates to your sewing machine that you've finished your current task, enabling you to easily position your next piece for stitching because the needle will consistently align and begin in the same position.

String Appliqué

When two or more appliqués are in close proximity on the same layer, I recommend stitching your first appliqué as instructed in "Stitching the Appliqués" on page 15, but instead of clipping the threads when you finish, lift the presser foot and slide the background to the next appliqué without lifting it from the sewing-machine surface. Lower the presser foot and resume stitching the next appliqué, remembering to end with a locking stitch. After the cluster of appliqués has been stitched, clip the threads between each.

Removing Paper Pattern Pieces

On the wrong side of the stitched appliqué, use embroidery scissors to carefully pinch and cut through the fabric at least ¼" inside the appliqué seam. Trim away the background fabric, leaving a generous ¼" seam allowance. Grasp the appliqué edge between the thumb and forefinger of one hand and the appliqué seam allowance with the other hand; give a gentle but firm tug to free the paper edge. Next, use your fingertip to loosen the glue anchoring the pattern piece to the fabric; peel away and discard the paper. Any paper that remains in the appliqué corners can be pulled out with a pair of tweezers.

Completing the Machine-Appliqué Process

Working from the bottom layer to the top, continue basting and stitching the appliqués until

each one has been secured in place, remembering to remove the paper pattern pieces before adding each new layer. Keep in mind that it isn't necessary to stitch any edge that will be overlapped by another piece. If needed, *briefly* press your finished work from the back to ensure the seam allowances lie smooth and flat. Always take care not to apply direct heat to the front of your appliqués, as this could weaken the monofilament threads.

Turn-Free Hand Appliqué

For an on-the-go option for your appliqué projects, the following technique will help you prepare projects that are portable. In addition to the items outlined in "Invisible Machine Appliqué" on page 11, you'll need the following supplies:

- Fine-gauge thread in a variety of colors to match your appliqués
- Straw appliqué needles (size 9 or 10 work well for me)
- Thimble

To prepare and stitch the appliqués, follow these steps.

1. After preparing the appliqués using freezer paper as outlined in "Invisible Machine Appliqué" on page 11, lay them out on the background to ensure everything fits and is to your liking. Remove all but the bottom pieces and baste the remaining appliqués in place as instructed in "Basting Appliqués" on page 15.

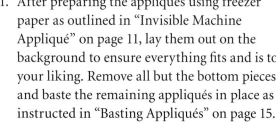
2. Cut a length of thread in a color to match the appliqué and use it to thread the needle. Form a small loop near the tail end of the thread to tie a knot, rolling it between your thumb and forefinger two or three times to draw the end through the opening. Bring the threaded needle up from the wrong side of the background, just inside the appliqué, catching two or three threads along the edge and pulling until the knot is flush with the fabric.

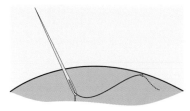

3. Insert the needle into the background just behind the point where the thread exits the fabric and come back up through the appliqué a tiny distance in front of your last stitch, again just catching the threads along the edge; gently pull the thread until the stitch is secure. Continue stitching around the appliqué, taking

close, tiny stitches to secure it well; I suggest placing two stitches into all points to secure them well.

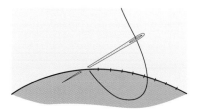

4. When you return to your starting point, bring the needle out on the wrong side of the background. Take two or three small backstitches just inside the appliqué edge, drawing the thread through the loop each time to secure it and keep it hidden from the front without creating a shadow effect.

5. Clip the thread tail and remove the paper pattern piece as instructed in "Removing Paper Pattern Pieces" on page 17.

6. Continue working from the bottom layer to the top to stitch the remaining appliqués, remembering to remove the paper pattern pieces before adding each new layer.

Fusible Appliqué

For quickly completed appliqué projects that are suitable for any skill level, the following fusible technique works beautifully. In addition to standard quiltmaking supplies, you'll need the following items for this method:

- All-purpose sewing thread in a complementary neutral color, or individual colors to match your appliqués

- Freezer paper
- Paper-backed iron-on adhesive (I like the results achieved with HeatnBond Lite)
- Sewing machine capable of producing a satin stitch

One point to remember when you're working with appliqués prepared from an iron-on adhesive is that your finished shapes will appear backward and be reversed on your quilt if they are directional and aren't perfectly symmetrical. Making a pattern template and remembering to reverse its direction as you begin preparing your appliqués will enable you to duplicate the design accurately. To prepare and stitch the fusible appliqués, follow these steps.

1. Trace each appliqué shape the number of times indicated in the pattern instructions onto the paper side of your iron-on adhesive, leaving approximately ½" between each shape. For projects with numerous identical shapes (or non-symmetrical shapes that need to be reversed), make a template as instructed in "Preparing Pattern Templates" on page 12 and use it to trace the required number of pieces. Remember that for this method you'll need one traced shape for each appliqué.

2. Cut out each shape approximately ¼" *outside* the drawn lines, and then cut away the center portion of the shape approximately ¼" *inside* the drawn lines to eliminate bulk and keep the shape pliable after the appliqué has been stitched.

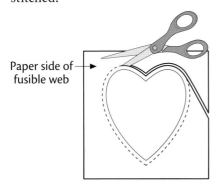

Paper side of fusible web →

Cutting line →

PIN POINT

Stabilizing Large Pattern Pieces Cut from Fusible Web

For added stability in large appliqué shapes cut from an iron-on adhesive, I recommend leaving a narrow strip of paper across the middle of the shape as you cut away the excess center portion; this strip will act as a bridge to connect the sides and it will be easier to lay the shape onto your fabric without distortion.

3. Following the manufacturer's instructions, fuse each shape, paper side *up*, to the *wrong* side of the fabric. After the fabric has cooled, cut out each shape exactly on the drawn lines. To protect the fusible adhesive and prevent the fabric appliqué edges from fraying, I leave the paper backing on my prepared pieces until I'm ready to use them. To remove the paper backing, loosen an inside edge of the paper and peel it away.

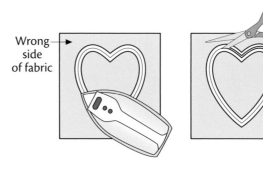

Wrong side of fabric →

4. Lay out the appliqués to ensure everything fits and is to your liking; remove all but the bottom appliqués. Following the manufacturer's instructions, fuse the appliqués to the background, working from the bottom layer to the top and overlapping any piece that rests upon another approximately ¼".

5. Thread the sewing machine with neutral thread or a color to match or complement your appliqué. Set the machine to a narrow satin stitch and sew each appliqué in place, beginning with the bottom pieces and working to the top. Ensure that you overlap the starting and stopping points of each stitched piece by about ⅛".

When I use a satin stitch for my fusible projects, I love the look achieved when my inner stitches land three or four threads inside the appliqué edge and the outer stitches land in the background exactly next to the appliqué—this width of about 1⁄16" is enough to encase the raw appliqué edges without resulting in a heavy look. I recommend fine-tuning your stitch by experimenting on a practice piece, and then noting your settings on your sample for future reference.

Wool Appliqué

Wool is a really fun, fast, and forgiving fabric to work with, and I especially love the magic that happens when it's used in combination with traditional cotton fabrics. Wool that's been felted has a soft, densely woven feel to the cloth and it resists raveling as you work with it. I suggest that you use only 100% wool and, as a general rule, avoid worsted wool because it doesn't felt well and can be challenging to work with. You can usually identify worsted wool by its hard, flat weave, and you'll often find it used for garments such as men's suits.

For my method of appliquéing with wool, you'll need the following items in addition to your standard quiltmaking supplies:

- #8 or #12 perle cotton in colors to match or complement wool
- Embroidery needle (a size 5 works well for me)
- Freezer paper
- Liquid fabric-basting glue, water soluble and acid free (my favorite brand is Quilter's Choice Basting Glue by Beacon Adhesives)
- Paper-backed iron-on adhesive (I like the results achieved when using HeatnBond Lite)
- Sharp scissors with a fine point
- Thimble

Felting Your Wool

If your wool hasn't been felted, this is easy to do. Wash similar-hued wool pieces in the washing machine on the longest cycle using a hot water wash and a cold water rinse. (You may wish to skim the surface of the water once or twice during the cycle to prevent loose fibers from clogging the drain.) Next, dry the wool in your dryer, again using the longest and hottest setting. Remove the dry wool promptly to help prevent wrinkles from forming.

As an added safety measure, I always wash and dry vividly colored pieces separately when I suspect they might lose dye, and I never wash wool that has been over dyed, since it will almost certainly bleed color—if I'm not sure whether a piece has been over dyed, I follow the rule that it's better to be safe and ask rather than to guess and be sorry. Finally, never wash wool that's been included as part of a kitted project, because it can continue to shrink and you may find yourself without enough wool to complete your project.

Preparing Wool Appliqués

I prepare my wool appliqués using the steps outlined in "Fusible Appliqué" on page 18 and glue baste them for stitching as described in "Basting Appliqués" on page 15, removing the paper backing of each prepared piece as it's used and applying small dots of liquid glue directly onto the narrow margin of fusible adhesive that rims each shape. For wool designs that contain multiple layers, I work from the top layer to the bottom to glue baste, heat set, and stitch each new piece as it's added, and then add these joined pieces to the background as a single unit. Heat setting prepared wool layers from the back will help them adhere better, so for this reason, always wait to remove the paper backing on any wool piece that will come into direct contact with the iron until *after* it has been heat set; the paper backing should be removed from all wool pieces prior to stitching them to the background.

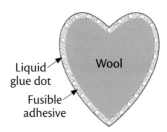

Liquid glue dot

Wool

Fusible adhesive

The combination of the fusible adhesive and the liquid glue produces ideal results because the iron-on adhesive finishes and stabilizes the underside of the wool edges to reduce fraying, while the glue-basted edges hold the layers of wool together beautifully for easy stitching without pinning. Keep in mind when you're working with wool appliqués in this manner that your finished shapes will appear backward and be reversed on your quilt if they are directional and aren't perfectly symmetrical. Making a pattern template as outlined in "Preparing Pattern Templates" on page 12 and remembering to reverse its direction as you begin preparing your appliqués will enable you to duplicate the design accurately.

Stitching Wool Appliqués

After much experimenting, I've decided that the overhand stitch is my preferred method of appliquéing wool shapes because it's quick, uses less thread, provides a softer look than the blanket stitch, and the stitches stay put without rolling.

Whenever possible, I work from the top layer to the bottom to stitch any layered wool pieces into units (such as a stack of pennies) *before*

PIN POINT

Stitching Styles

Traditionally, wool appliqués are sewn using a blanket stitch, but my personal preference is to use an overhand stitch because it's quicker to sew, uses less thread, the finished stitches have a more subtle appearance, and the outer line of stitching will not roll away from the appliqué edges as can sometimes happen with a blanket stitch.

Overhand stitches are commonly worked from the outer edge of the shape inward (as shown in the illustration at right), and we strive for straight, even stitches. If you find that your overhand stitches consistently have a bit of a slant to them, you may have better success using the same stitch but reversing the direction of your sewing to work from the *inside* of your shape *outward*, as I do. When sewing my overhand stitches, I lightly draw my needle over the appliqué surface straight down from the point where my thread exits the cloth at the appliqué edge, and then move it backward about a thread's width before inserting it and bringing it back up along the appliqué edge approximately ⅛" to ¼" in front of my previous stitch. Adjusting the entry point of my inner stitch back about a thread's width helps to compensate for the slant that can occur when my stitches are pulled tight, resulting in finished stitches that look straight and true.

adding them to my background, because this simplifies the sewing process and eliminates the need to stitch through multiple heavy layers of wool. Once the layered units have been sewn together, the appliqué designs can be stitched to the background, working from the bottom layer to the top.

1. Lay out your appliqués, including any stitched appliqué units, onto your background to ensure everything fits and is to your liking. Remove all but the bottom pieces and glue baste them in place, referring to "Basting Appliqués" on page 15. Use an embroidery needle threaded with a single knotted strand of #8 or #12 perle cotton to overhand stitch the pieces in place as shown in "Decorative Stitches" below.

2. Lay out, baste, and stitch the next layer of appliqués, ensuring that any appliqué overlapping another piece does so by at least ¼". Continue working from the bottom layer to the top to complete the appliqué design, keeping in mind that it isn't necessary to cut away the backs of any appliqués stitched from wool.

Decorative Stitches

Decorative stitches can be used to beautifully embellish your work, and some can even be functional when used during the assembly of your projects. All of the stitches shown below are stitched with a single strand of knotted thread. You'll find the suggested types of thread and needle sizes in the individual pattern instructions.

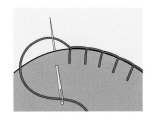

Blanket stitch

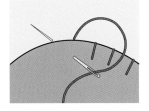

Overhand stitch

French knot

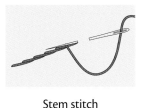

Stem stitch

PIN POINT

Stitched Leaves with Style

For a polished look for the points of my wool leaf appliqués (and other shapes featuring points), I take my last stitch prior to reaching the point, and then bring my needle up directly at the point just outside the appliqué edge. Next, I insert the needle back into the leaf at the inner point of my last stitch and bring it up on the opposite outside edge of the leaf to form a mirror image. I finish the stitch by inserting the needle back into the inner point where the stitches converge, and then continue stitching along the unsewn edge of the leaf.

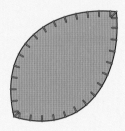

Completing the Quilt Top

Once the individual components of your quilt have been finished, assembling everything and adding your borders is the next step. The information that follows will help simplify and streamline this process.

Assembling the Quilt Center

Lay out your blocks or units, evaluating their placement and making any necessary changes; I suggest positioning blocks or units with strong hues into your corners to visually anchor and define the quilt center.

For greater ease when assembling large tops, join the rows in groups of two or three. Next, join the grouped rows, working from the top and bottom edges toward the middle until you join all the rows.

Adding Borders

When joining border strips to the center of a quilt, fold each border piece in half to find the midpoint, and then finger-press a crease. Next fold each side of the quilt center and crease these midpoint positions as well. Align the creases of your individual components and pin them together for a perfect fit.

All of the measurements provided in this book for whole-cloth borders are mathematically correct, but because there is little or no stretch to these pieces when they've been cut from the lengthwise grain, you may wish to slightly increase the designated lengths. I routinely increase the length of my strips by ½" for borders measuring up to 60" long and by 1" for strips in excess of 60"; any excess length can be trimmed after the borders are added.

Finishing Techniques

There are many choices available as you work through the final steps of your project—tailoring these decisions to suit your individual preferences will result in a finished quilt that's yours alone.

Batting

For quilt tops sewn from prewashed fabrics, I suggest using polyester batting because it will ensure minimal shrinkage when your quilt is laundered. If your quilt top was stitched from fabrics that weren't prewashed, I'd recommend choosing cotton batting, particularly if you love the slightly puckered look of vintage quilts. Regardless of your choice, always follow the manufacturer's instructions for the very best results.

Backing

I cut and piece my quilt backings to be approximately 3" larger than my quilt top on all sides. As you consider your backing fabric choices, remember that prints with a lot of texture will make your quilting less visible, while muted prints and solids will emphasize your quilting design. To prevent shadowing, use fabrics in colors similar to those in your quilt top.

For the best use of yardage, seam your quilt backings as shown.

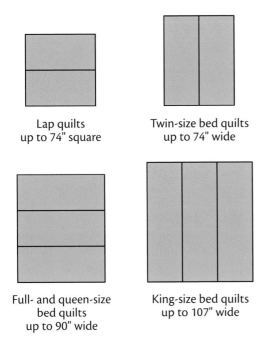

Lap quilts
up to 74" square

Twin-size bed quilts
up to 74" wide

Full- and queen-size
bed quilts
up to 90" wide

King-size bed quilts
up to 107" wide

Basting

To prepare your finished top for the quilting process:

1. Place the backing fabric, wrong side up, on a large, flat surface. Smooth away any wrinkles and secure the edges with masking tape.
2. Center the batting on the backing fabric and smooth away any wrinkles.
3. Carefully center the quilt top on the layered batting and backing.
- For hand quilting, use white thread to baste from corner to corner, and then at 3" to 4" intervals as shown.
- For pin basting, use size 2 rustproof safety pins and work from the center outward at 4" to 5" intervals as shown. Last, thread baste the edges.

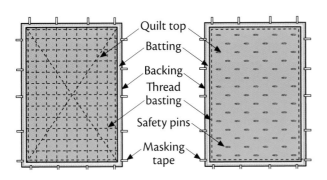

Quilt top
Batting
Backing
Thread basting
Safety pins
Masking tape

A Handy Holder for Scissors

If you're at all like me and are constantly losing your scissors, try this little trick. Follow the manufacturer's instructions to apply a 3-M hook to the side surface of your sewing machine or an adjacent wall . . . or, throw restraint completely out the window and attach a hook to both! Hang a pair of scissors on your new holder, and they'll never be lost again.

Marking Quilting Designs

A quick and easy way to mark straight quilting lines is to use masking tape in various widths as a stitching guide, but always remember to remove the tape at the end of each day to prevent adhesive from damaging your fabric. More elaborate designs can be marked onto the top using a quilter's pencil or a fine-tipped water-soluble marker—doing this before the layers are assembled will provide a smooth marking surface and produce the best results. For a beautiful finish, always ensure your quilt features an abundant and evenly spaced amount of quilting.

Hand Quilting

To hand quilt your project, place the layered quilt top in a hoop or frame and follow these steps:

1. Thread your needle with an approximately 18" length of quilting thread and knot one end. Insert the needle into the quilt top about 1" from where you wish to begin quilting, sliding it through the layers and bringing it up through the top; gently tug until the knot is drawn down into the layer of batting.
2. Sew small, even stitches through the layers until you near the end of the thread. Make a knot in the thread about ⅛" from the quilt top. Insert and slide the needle through the batting layer, bringing it back up about 1" beyond your last stitch, tugging gently until the knot disappears; carefully clip the thread.

Hand-quilting stitch

Big-Stitch Quilting

Big-stitch quilting is one of my favorite methods because it's a quick way to include hand stitching on my projects without the huge time commitment that traditional hand quilting can require. For this style of quilting I use a size 5 embroidery needle and #8 or #12 perle cotton to sew a running stitch (with each stitch approximately ⅛" to a scant ¼" long) through the quilt layers, ending my stitches as I would for traditional hand quilting.

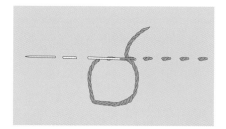

Machine Quilting

For in-depth machine-quilting instructions, please refer to *Machine Quilting Made Easy!* by Maurine Noble (Martingale & Company, 1994).

When an overall style of quilting is my best choice to add subtle texture without introducing another design element into my project mix, I use a swirling pattern.

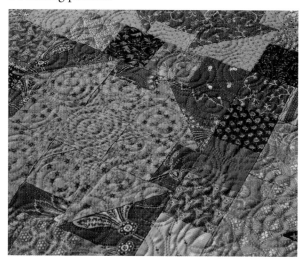

To stitch this versatile design, sew a free-form circle of any size, and then fill in the center with ever-reducing concentric circles (think cinnamon rolls). When you arrive at the center, stitch a gentle wavy line to the next area to be swirled and continue filling the block or top, staggering the placement and size of the swirls, until the stitching is complete.

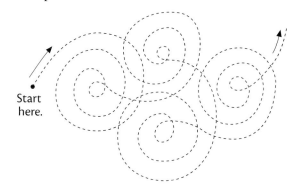

Start here.

Binding

Traditionally, a 2½"-wide French-fold binding is used to finish most quilts. When I bind my quilts, however, I prefer a more unconventional method using 2"-wide strips that results in a traditional look from the front while producing a "chubby" border of color to frame the backing in a more striking manner. The binding yardage for each project will accommodate either method, with enough binding to encircle the quilt perimeter plus approximately 10" for mitered corners.

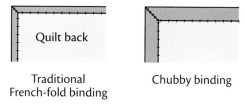

Quilt back

Traditional French-fold binding

Chubby binding

Traditional French-Fold Binding

1. With right sides together, join the 2½"-wide strips end to end at right angles, stitching diagonally across the corners, to make one long strip. Trim the seam allowances to ¼" and press them open.

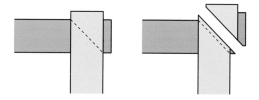

2. Cut one end at a 45° angle and press it under ¼". Fold the strip in half lengthwise, with wrong sides together, and press.

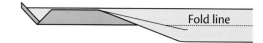

Fold line

3. Beginning along one side of the quilt top, not a corner, use a ¼" seam allowance to stitch the binding along the raw edges. Stop sewing ¼" from the first corner and backstitch. Clip the thread and remove the quilt from under the presser foot.

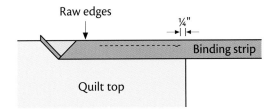

Raw edges

¼"

Binding strip

Quilt top

4. Make a fold in the binding, bringing it up and back down onto itself to square the corner. Rotate the quilt 90° and reposition it under the presser foot. Resume sewing at the top edge of the quilt, continuing around the perimeter in this manner.

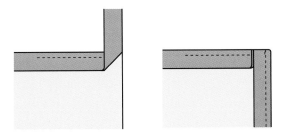

5. When you approach your starting point, cut the binding end at an angle 1" longer than needed and tuck it inside the previously sewn binding to enclose the raw end. Complete the stitching.

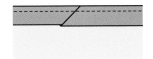

6. Bring the folded edge of the binding to the back of the quilt, enclosing the raw edges. Use a blind stitch and matching thread to hand sew the binding to the back. At each corner, fold the binding to form a miter and stitch it in place.

Chubby Binding

For this method, you'll need a bias-tape maker designed to produce 1"-wide, double-fold tape. For most of my quilts, I prefer to use binding strips that have been cut on the straight of grain, rather than the bias, because I feel this gives my quilt edges more stability. For scrappy bindings pieced from many prints of different lengths, I join the strips end to end using straight seams and start with a straight fold at the beginning.

1. Cut the strips 2" wide and join them end to end. Next, slide the pieced strip through the bias-tape maker, pressing the folds with a hot, dry iron as they emerge so the raw edges meet in the center. As the tape maker slides along the pieced strip, the seams will automatically be directed to one side as they are pressed.

2. Open the fold of the strip along the top edge only. Turn the beginning raw end under ½" and finger-press the fold. Starting along one side of the quilt top, not a corner, align the unfolded raw edge of the binding with the raw edge of the quilt and stitch as instructed in steps 3 and 4 of the French-fold method at left.

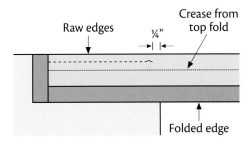

Crease from top fold

Raw edges

¼"

Folded edge

3. When you approach your starting point, cut the end to extend 1" beyond the folded edge and complete the stitching.

4. Bring the folded edge of the binding to the back and hand stitch it (including the mitered folds at the corners) as instructed in step 6 of the French-fold method at left. The raw end of the strip will now be encased within the binding.

Attaching a Quilt Label

To document your work, remember to prepare a fabric quilt label including any information you'd like to share, and then hand stitch it to the back of your quilt.

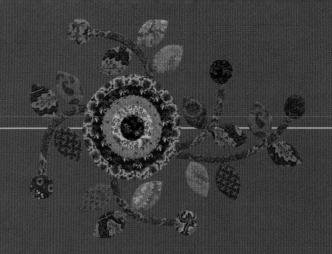

COTTAGE GARDEN

Like pennies in a sparkling fountain, these colorful appliqué circles seem to cast off little ripples of happiness as they land on this cozy and inviting patchwork table runner. Make a wish, and then scatter some pennies of your own.

Materials

⅞ yard *total* of assorted neutral prints for blocks and sashing strips

¾ yard *total* of assorted print scraps, approximately 6" x 6" and smaller, for penny appliqués, and enough 2½"-wide random-length strips to make a 104" length of binding when joined end to end

1 fat eighth (9" x 22") of light brown print for blocks and setting squares

1 fat eighth of green print for stem and leaf appliqués

Assorted scraps of green prints for leaf appliqués

1 yard of fabric for backing

18" x 52" rectangle of batting

Bias bar

#8 or #12 perle cotton

Size 5 embroidery needle

Finished quilt: 12½" x 46½"
Finished blocks: 10" x 10"
Designed, machine pieced, machine appliquéd, and hand quilted in the big-stitch method by Kim Diehl.

Cutting

Cut all pieces across the width of the fabric unless otherwise noted. Refer to page 35 for appliqué patterns A–F and to "Invisible Machine Appliqué" on page 11 for pattern preparation. Refer to "Cutting Bias Strips" on page 8 to cut bias strips.

From the assorted neutral prints, cut a *total* of:
3 squares, 4½" x 4½"
12 rectangles, 1½" x 4½"
12 rectangles, 1½" x 6½"
12 rectangles, 1½" x 8½"
10 rectangles, 1½" x 10½"
12 rectangles, 1½" x 12½"

From the light brown print, cut:
44 squares, 1½" x 1½"

From the *bias* of the green print fat eighth, cut:
12 rectangles, 1¼" x 5½"
2 rectangles, 1¼" x 8"

From the remainder of the green print, cut:
6 using pattern F

From the assorted print scraps, cut a *total* of:
3 *each* using patterns A, B, C, and D
17 using pattern E
Enough 2½"-wide random lengths to make a 104" length of binding when joined end to end

From the assorted green print scraps, cut a *total* of:
36 using pattern F

Piecing the Blocks

Sew all pieces with right sides together unless otherwise noted.

1. Sew the neutral print 1½" x 4½" rectangles to opposite sides of each neutral print 4½" square. Press the seam allowances toward the rectangles.

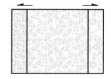

Make 3.

2. Join a brown print 1½" square to each end of the remaining neutral print 1½" x 4½" rectangles. Sew the resulting pieced rectangles to the remaining sides of the 4½" squares from step 1. Press the seam allowances toward the pieced rectangles.

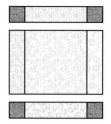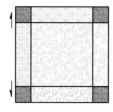

3. Repeat steps 1 and 2 to add the neutral print 1½" x 6½" rectangles, and then the neutral print 1½" x 8½" rectangles to the previous unit to complete the blocks.

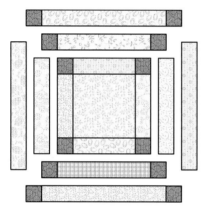

Make 3.

Assembling the Table Runner

1. Referring to the table runner assembly diagram, lay out the three pieced blocks in alternating positions with four assorted neutral print 1½" x 10½" rectangles. Join the pieces. Press the seam allowances away from the pieced blocks.

2. Lay out three assorted neutral print 1½" x 10½" rectangles in alternating positions with four light brown print 1½" squares. Join the pieces. Press the seam allowances toward the rectangles. Repeat for a total of two pieced sashing rows. Join these rows to the long sides of the table runner. Press the seam allowances toward the sashing rows.

PIN POINT

Pennies for Embellishing

The penny shapes in the "Cottage Garden Table Runner" are so versatile and fast to prepare that they can be used to embellish any number of items. I used a purchased 20" x 28" kitchen towel, raided my scrap basket, and then used the "Fusible Appliqué" method on page 18 to stitch this quick project. Add some decorative machine stitching to trail along the hemmed edge, and this little towel is almost too sweet to use.

3. Join six assorted neutral print 1½" x 12½" rectangles to make a pieced unit. Press the seam allowances in one direction. Repeat for a total of two pieced units. Join these units to opposite ends of the table runner. Press the seam allowances away from the table runner center. The table runner top should now measure 12½" x 46½", including the seam allowances.

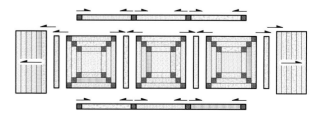

4. Fold each narrow end of the table runner top in half and finger-press a crease at the center position. Use an acrylic ruler and pencil to draw a diagonal line from each outermost light brown print square to the creased outer edge of the table runner. (The fabric outside these marked points will be trimmed away after the appliqué is completed.)

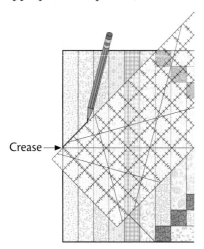

Crease →

Appliquéing the Table Runner

1. Prepare each of the green print 1¼"-wide rectangles as instructed in "Making Bias-Tube Stems and Vines" on page 14.
2. Center a prepared A penny appliqué over the center square of each pieced block; pin in place. Referring to "Basting Appliqués" on page 15 and using the quilt photo as a guide, lay out four prepared 5½"-long stems on

each block, tucking the raw ends under the A circles approximately ¼". In the same manner, position a prepared 8"-long stem on each outer block, ensuring the stems lie well within the marked triangular areas. Lay out and baste the leaves, positioning them as shown. Remove the A appliqués.
3. Referring to "Stitching the Appliqués" on page 15, stitch the basted stems and leaves in place. Remove the paper pattern pieces as instructed in "Removing Paper Pattern Pieces" on page 17.
4. Working from the bottom layer to the top, lay out, baste, and stitch the remaining A, B, C, D, and E penny appliqués, remembering to remove the paper pattern pieces before adding each new layer.

Completing the Table Runner

Trim away the excess background cloth exactly on the drawn lines at the ends of the table runner. Refer to "Finishing Techniques" on page 22 and "Big-Stitch Quilting" on page 24 for details as needed. Layer the quilt top, batting, and backing. Quilt the layers. The featured quilt was hand quilted in the big-stitch method, with the appliqués outlined to emphasize their shapes and Xs quilted on the light brown squares. The neutral strips were quilted in the ditch along the seam lines. Join the assorted print 2½"-wide random lengths into a 104"-long strip and use it to bind the quilt.

COTTAGE GARDEN PENNY MUG MATS

Finished size: approximately 4¼" in diameter

Materials (for one mug mat)

Scraps of four assorted prints, approximately
    5" x 5" and smaller, for pennies
1 square, 5" x 5", of fabric for backing
1 square, 5" x 5", of cotton batting
Water-soluble marker
Dritz spray adhesive
#8 or #12 perle cotton
Size 5 embroidery needle

Making the Mug Mat

1. Referring to "Invisible Machine Appliqué"
   on page 11, use the assorted print scraps to
   prepare one *each* of patterns B, C, D, and E on
   page 35; do not press the seam allowance of
   the B appliqué onto the paper pattern piece,
   but instead use a water-soluble marker to trace
   exactly along the paper edge on the wrong
   side of the fabric. Remove and set aside the B
   pattern piece.
2. Work from the bottom layer to the top to
   position and appliqué the C, D, and E shapes
   onto the center of the B circle, remembering to
   remove the paper pattern pieces before adding
   each new layer.
3. Use a water-soluble marker and the set-aside B
   pattern piece to trace a circle onto the batting
   square; cut out the circle on the inside of the
   drawn line. Apply spray adhesive to the circle
   of batting and affix it to the wrong side of
   the appliquéd B unit from step 2, centering it
   within the traced circle.
4. With right sides together, layer the prepared B
   unit onto the backing square; pin in place. Cut
   the backing flush with the edge of the B unit;

machine stitch the layers together along the traced line, beginning and ending with a back stitch and leaving an opening about 1½" wide for turning.

5. Turn the mug mat right side out, ensuring the outer edges are smooth and round, and carefully press the mat edges flat; use a needle and matching thread to hand stitch the opening closed. Add big-stitch quilting around the outside edge of the inner pennies. Referring to "Blanket Stitch" on page 21, finish the mug mat edge, sliding the needle through the layers as you sew to keep the stitches visible from the front only.

COTTAGE GARDEN EMBELLISHED LAMP SHADE

Materials

Lamp shade, approximately 8½" tall, with a base of approximately 12" in diameter
Assorted wool scraps (including green), approximately 6" x 6" and smaller, for appliqués
½ yard of HeatnBond Lite iron-on adhesive
Dritz spray adhesive
Awl or stiletto with sharp point
#8 or #12 perle cotton
Size 7 embroidery needle

Cutting

Refer to page 35 for appliqué patterns A–F and to "Preparing Wool Appliqués" on page 20, for pattern-piece preparation.

From the assorted wool scraps, cut a *total* of:
4 *each* using patterns A, B, and C
8 *each* using patterns D and E
24 using pattern F

Appliquéing the Lamp Shade

Keep in mind that it's easy to adapt this pattern to ensure it perfectly fits your lampshade. By adding or subtracting appliqué circles to the leaf-framed penny units, you can increase or decrease the design size to personalize the fit.

1. Referring to "Stitching Wool Appliqués" on page 21, stitch four layered large penny units containing an A, B, C, D, and E appliqué and four layered small penny units containing one each of the D and E appliqués.

2. Apply spray adhesive to the wrong side of a large penny unit and press it onto the lamp shade, centering it approximately between the top and bottom edges. Cut and lay a piece of string over the top of the shade, with one end extending down onto the center of the penny unit and the other end extending down exactly opposite; use this string position to press a second prepared large penny unit onto the shade. Affix the remaining two large penny units onto the shade, centering them between the first units. Last, prepare and press the small penny units onto the shade, centering them between the large units.

3. Use an awl to carefully pierce the shade around the appliqué edges from the front, placing these tiny pilot holes for stitching approximately ¼" apart. Referring to "Decorative Stitches" on page 21, overhand stitch the outer edges of the appliqués to the shade using the pierced holes as a stitching guide. As you approach the end of your perle cotton or wish to end a finished piece, knot the thread just beyond the length of your anticipated last stitch and slide the needle between the wool and the lamp shade, bringing it up about 1" away; gently pull until the knot disappears and clip the thread.

4. Referring to the lamp shade photo, prepare, position, and overhand stitch the leaves.

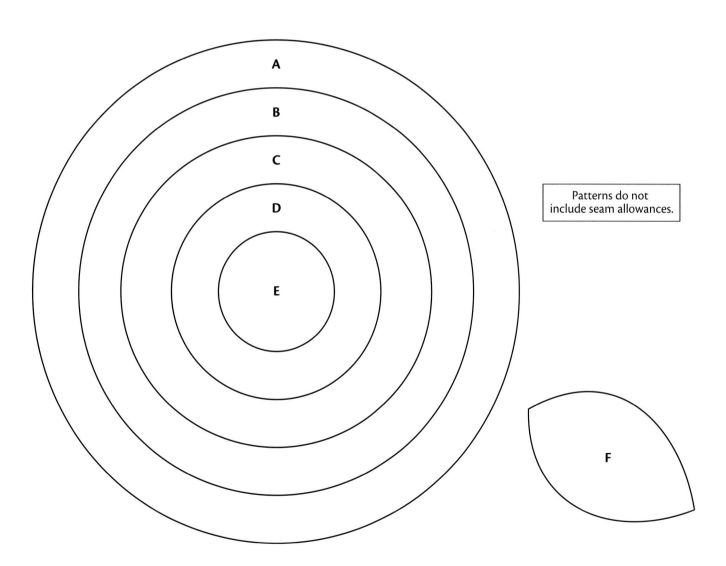

Patterns do not
include seam allowances.

BITTERSWEET BRIAR

Flirty red petals, twining vines, and sprays of bittersweet berries are the perfect recipe for making any room merry and bright. Hang this little quilt where you'll see it often, and each glance will be sure to bring a smile.

Materials

2 yards of neutral striped fabric for block and
   border background
1¾ yards of medium green print for vines,
   appliqués, border patchwork, and binding
4 fat quarters (18" x 22") of assorted red prints for
   large center petal appliqués
16 chubby sixteenths (9" x 11") of assorted prints
   for appliqués
1 fat quarter of cheddar-colored print for berry
   appliqués
3 yards of fabric for backing
54" x 54" square of batting
Bias bar

Cutting

Cut all pieces across the width of the fabric unless otherwise noted. Refer to pages 47–49 for appliqué patterns A–J and to "Invisible Machine Appliqué" on page 11 for pattern piece preparation. Refer to "Cutting Bias Strips" on page 8 to cut bias strips.

From the neutral striped fabric, cut:
4 squares, 20½" x 20½" (or 1 square, 40½" x 40½", if you use print fabric)
5 strips, 4½" x 42"; crosscut into 40 squares, 4½" x 4½"

From the medium green print, cut:
5 strips, 4½" x 42"; crosscut into:
    20 rectangles, 4½" x 8½"
    4 squares, 4½" x 4½"
5 strips, 2½" x 42" (binding)

From the *bias* of the remaining medium green print, cut:
Enough 1½"-wide strips to equal 4 lengths, 45" each, when joined using straight, not diagonal, seams

From the scraps of the medium green print, cut:
16 using a random mix of patterns I and I reversed
8 using pattern H

From *each* of the 4 assorted red print fat quarters, cut:
1 using pattern A (4 total)

From the leftover red print and the 16 assorted print chubby sixteenths, cut a *total* of:
12 using pattern B
1 *each* using patterns C and D
25 using pattern E
4 *each* using patterns F and G

From the fat quarter of cheddar-colored print, cut:
52 using pattern J

Piecing and Appliquéing the Quilt Center

Sew all pieces with right sides together unless otherwise noted.

1. Lay out four neutral striped 20½" squares in two horizontal rows of two squares each as shown. Join the squares in each row. Press the seam allowances of each row in opposite directions. Join the rows. Press the seam allowances to one side. The pieced quilt center should measure 40½" square, including the seam allowances. (If you are using a neutral print 40½" square for the quilt center, fold it in half, right sides together, and lightly press center vertical and horizontal creases.)

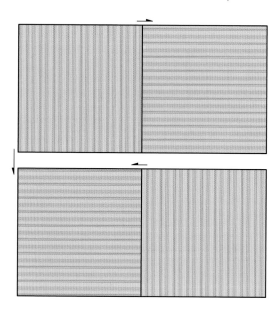

2. Referring to "Making Bias-Tube Stems and Vines" on page 14, prepare the four medium green print 45" lengths. Cut *each* prepared vine into one 24" length, one 16" length, and one 4" length. You will have a total of four vines in each of the designated lengths.

Finished quilt: 48½" x 48½" • **Finished quilt center:** 40" x 40"
Designed, machine pieced, machine appliquéd, and hand quilted in the big-stitch method by Kim Diehl.

3. Position the prepared A appliqués onto the pieced background, placing them diagonally with the outer points of the bottom raw edges resting against the vertical and horizontal seams (or pressed creases) near the center. Referring to "Basting Appliqués" on page 15, baste in place.

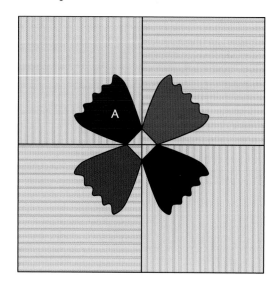

4. Fold and finger-press a center vertical and horizontal crease into the prepared C appliqué; align these creases with the background seams to perfectly center the circle and ensure it overlaps the raw edges of the A appliqués by approximately ¼"; remove the C appliqué. Referring to "Stitching the Appliqués" on page 15, stitch the A appliqués in place. Remove the paper pattern pieces as instructed in "Removing Paper Pattern Pieces" on page 17.

5. Position, baste, and stitch three B appliqués onto each A appliqué, angling the two outer pieces so they flair slightly outward to follow the petal shape; the inner raw points of the

angled B appliqués should be flush with the raw edges of the petals with outer-most points resting below these raw edges. Remove the paper pattern pieces.

6. Referring to the quilt photo, lay out and baste a 24" main stem, placing the bottom raw end flush with the bottom raw edges of the A appliqués. Add a 16" stem to be used for the berries, positioning the raw end well underneath the 24" stem where they intersect.

PIN POINT

Tips for Placing Your Stems

I found it was much easier to have a target to "aim" for as I laid out my main stem, rather than guessing where it belonged on a sea of open background. To do this, I placed one of the large F flower appliqués onto the background cloth, positioning it about 3" out from the second left-hand outer curve of the red A petal. This, along with the built-in registration marks provided by the seams in the quilt center, helped me to uniformly duplicate the placement of my stems. To easily lay out the very curvy 16" stem, glue baste it well and press it down onto the cloth with one hand as you curve it into place with the other.

Last, lay out and baste a 4" stem. (Keep in mind as you lay out your stems that any excess length can be trimmed away to achieve the look you desire.) Repeat with the remaining three sets of stems. Lay out and baste four random I appliqués along each stem. Appliqué the stems and leaves in place.

7. Working from the bottom layer to the top, position, baste, and stitch one C, D, and E appliqué to the center of the flower, remembering to remove the paper pattern pieces before adding each new layer.

8. Referring to the quilt photo, position and baste a prepared F flower appliqué about ½" out from the tip of each 24" stem; appliqué in place and remove the paper pattern pieces. Work from the bottom layer to the top to continue positioning, basting, and stitching the G and H appliqués, ensuring the raw stem ends are well covered.

9. Work from the bottom layer to the top to position, baste, and stitch a prepared E and H appliqué to the tip of each 4" stem.

10. Lay out, baste, and stitch 13 J appliqués along each 16" stem, ensuring that one berry covers the raw end of each stem. Remove the paper pattern pieces.

Piecing and Appliquéing the Border

1. Using a pencil and acrylic ruler, lightly draw a diagonal line on the wrong side of each neutral striped 4½" square, positioning the direction of the stripes randomly.

2. Layer a prepared square over one end of a medium green print 4½" x 8½" rectangle as shown; stitch the pair together on the drawn line. Press and trim as instructed in "Pressing Triangle Units" on page 10. Repeat for a total of 20 pieced rectangles. In the same manner, stitch, press, and trim a second prepared neutral 4½" square onto the open end of each pieced rectangle, placing it in a mirror-image position.

Make 20.

3. Lay out five pieced rectangles from step 2, placing them end to end. Join the rectangles. Press each seam allowance to one side, whichever will result in the best point. Repeat for a total of four pieced border strips measuring 4½" x 40½", including the seam allowances.

Make 4.

4. Fold each of the remaining prepared E appliqués in half and finger-press a center crease. Select a pieced border strip from step 3. Position and baste four creased E appliqués onto the seamed neutral background between each green triangle, aligning the creases with the patchwork seams to center them and positioning them approximately 1¼" up from the neutral point. Stitch the appliqués in place and remove the paper pattern pieces. Repeat for a total of four appliquéd border strips.

1¼"   Make 4.

5. With right sides together, finger-press a vertical and horizontal center crease in each medium green print 4½" square. In the same manner, finger-press a second crease in the remaining E appliqués. Align the creases of an E appliqué with the creases of a green print square to perfectly center it. Baste and stitch the appliqué in place; remove the paper pattern piece. Repeat for a total of four appliquéd green squares.

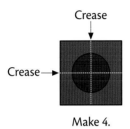

Crease

Crease →

Make 4.

Adding the Borders

1. Join the green edge of an appliquéd border strip to the right and left sides of the quilt center. Carefully press the seam allowances toward the quilt center, taking care not to apply heat to the appliqués.

2. Join an appliquéd green print 4½" square to each end of the remaining border strips. Carefully press the seam allowance toward the green square. Join these pieced strips to the remaining sides of the quilt center. Carefully press the seam allowances toward the quilt center. The pieced and appliquéd quilt top should now measure 48½" square, including the seam allowances.

Completing the Quilt

Refer to "Finishing Techniques" on page 22 for details as needed. Layer the quilt top, batting, and backing. Quilt the layers. The featured quilt was hand quilted in the big-stitch method, with lines stitched along the stripes of the center background fabric. Each appliqué was outlined for emphasis with a free-form curlicue line extending out from the skinny flower petals to the red print. The border patchwork was echo quilted in straight lines radiating out from the seams at regular intervals. Join the five green print 2½" x 42" strips into one length and use it to bind the quilt.

BITTERSWEET BRIAR
COTTON-AND-WOOL QUILT

Finished quilt size: 48½" x 48½" • Finished quilt center: 40" x 40"

Materials

2 yards of black striped cotton for block and border background*

1¾ yards of green cotton print for vines, border patchwork, and binding

4 squares, 11" x 11", of red wool for large A petal appliqués

12 rectangles, approximately 2" x 7", of assorted wool for B petal appliqués

25 squares, approximately 3" x 3", of assorted wool for E penny appliqués

2 squares, approximately 7" x 7" and smaller, of assorted wool for C and D penny appliqués

4 rectangles, approximately 5" x 7", of assorted wool for F blossom appliqués

4 rectangles, approximately 4" x 6", of assorted wool for G blossom appliqués

3 rectangles, approximately 8" x 10", of assorted green wool for H calyx appliqués and I leaf appliqués

1 square, approximately 12" x 12", or equivalent assorted scraps of cheddar-colored wool for J berry appliqués

3 yards of fabric for backing

54" x 54" square of batting

Bias bar

2 yards of HeatnBond Lite iron-on adhesive

#8 or #12 perle cotton

Size 5 embroidery needle

*If you choose to use a print rather than a striped fabric, purchase 1⅓ yards.

Cutting

1. Using the wool pieces and referring to "Materials" on page 43, cut out the appliqué pieces specified in "Cutting" on page 38.
2. Referring to "Cutting" on page 38, cut all cotton patchwork, stem, and binding pieces, using the black striped fabric and green prints specified for this project version.

Piecing and Appliquéing the Quilt Center

1. Sew the quilt center as instructed in step 1 of "Piecing and Appliquéing the Quilt Center" on page 38.
2. Referring to "Stitching Wool Appliqués" on page 21, prepare, position, and stitch three B appliqués to each A appliqué to make four red petal units. In the same manner, use a C, D, and E appliqué to stitch one penny unit. Last, prepare, layer, and stitch a G appliqué onto an F appliqué, repeating to make a total of four blossom units.
3. Referring to step 2 of "Piecing and Appliquéing the Quilt Center" on page 38, prepare the stems.
4. Position the red petal units onto the quilt center as instructed in steps 3 and 4 of "Piecing and Appliquéing the Quilt Center" on page 40. Baste the petal units in place, referring to "Basting Appliqués" on page 15. Referring to "Decorative Stitches" on page 21, overhand stitch them to the background.
5. Referring to step 6 of "Piecing and Appliquéing the Quilt Center" on page 40, lay out and appliqué the vines.
6. Using the quilt photo as a guide, lay out, baste, and overhand stitch the remaining quilt-center appliqués.

Completing the Project

1. Follow steps 1–5 of "Piecing and Appliquéing the Border" on page 41 to stitch and appliqué the border.
2. Refer to steps 1 and 2 of "Adding the Borders" on page 42 to add the borders to the quilt center.

3. Refer to "Finishing Techniques" on page 22 and "Big-Stitch Quilting" on page 24 for details as needed. Layer the quilt top, batting, and backing. Quilt the layers. The featured quilt was machine quilted with a pattern of teardrop shapes in the background areas and the patchwork borders were echo quilted. The wool appliqués were outlined with hand-sewn "big-stitch" quilting to emphasize their shapes. Join the five green print 2½" x 42" strips into one length and use it to bind the quilt.

PIN POINT

Balancing Act

As you're considering possible quilting designs for projects combining both cotton and wool, keep in mind that using an evenly spaced and moderate amount of quilting will help provide a good balance and compensate for the added weight and density of the wool.

BITTERSWEET BRIAR
FRAMED FRENCH KNOT MINIATURE

Finished size, unframed: 3¼" x 3¼"

Materials

One sheet of Printed Treasures by Milliken sew-on
    inkjet printable fabric
One rectangle, 8½" x 11", of lightweight fusible
    stabilizer
6-strand embroidery floss in assorted colors
Size 9 straw needle
6" embroidery hoop
Dritz spray adhesive
Picture frame with mat

Instructions

1. Using an inkjet printer and the sheet of Printed
   Treasures fabric, make a color photocopy of the
   4" Bittersweet Briar quilt illustration on page
   42, printing it onto the fabric side of the sheet.
   Carefully peel away the paper backing. Follow
   the manufacturer's instructions to iron fusible
   stabilizer onto the back of the printed fabric.
   Place the prepared design into an embroidery
   hoop.

2. Refer to "Decorative Stitches" on page 21 for details as needed. Beginning at the center of the design and working outward, use two strands of embroidery floss and the straw needle to densely fill in the design with French knots, matching the thread colors to the printed design. (For my project, I chose to omit the borders and feature only the center of this design.)

3. From the back, center the cardboard-weight backing piece from the frame onto the finished work and use a pencil to mark the edges on the fabric; trim away the excess fabric. Apply spray adhesive to the wrong side of the completed work and press it back in place onto the backing piece. Insert the mat and then the miniature into the frame.

PIN POINT

Instant Designs for Miniatures

The color illustrations in quilting books can provide you with an unlimited source of patterns for French knot and punchneedle projects. These small-scale designs will keep your fingers flying if you love hand work, and your pint-sized masterpieces can be framed and displayed on tabletops or tucked into the smallest niche for instant charm.

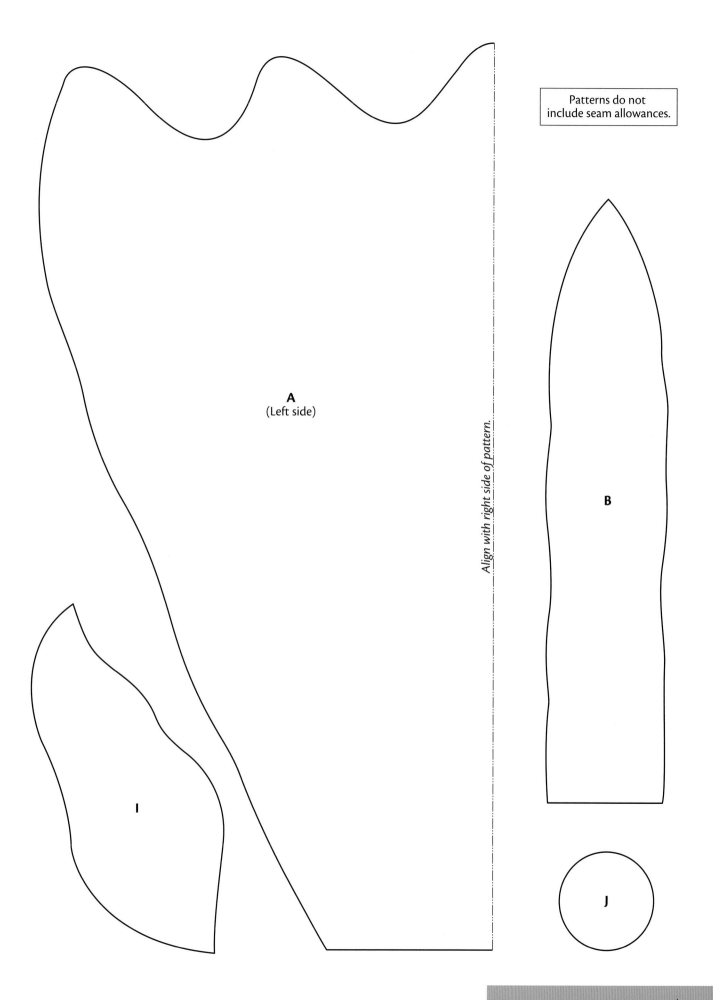

Patterns do not
include seam allowances.

A
(Left side)

Align with right side of pattern.

B

I

J

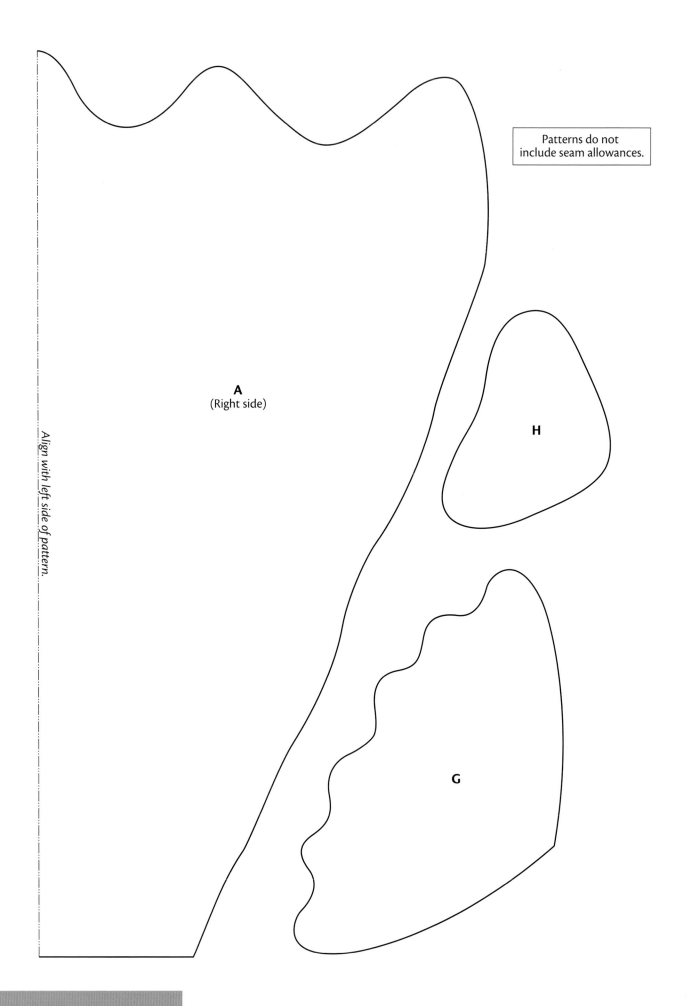

Patterns do not
include seam allowances.

A
(Right side)

Align with left side of pattern.

H

G

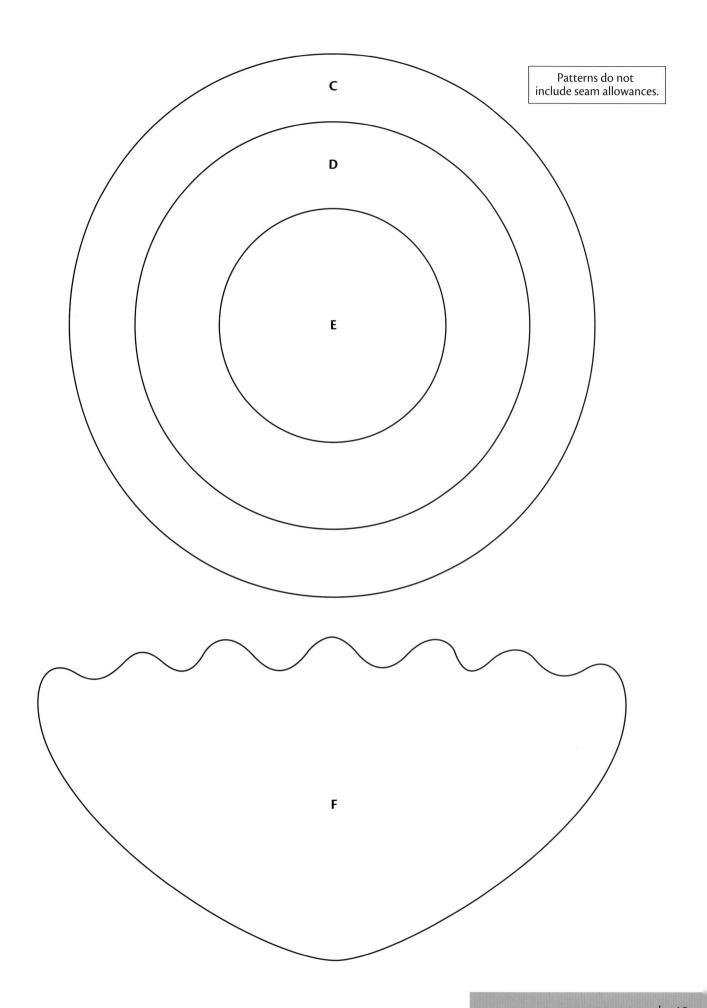

Patterns do not
include seam allowances.

C

D

E

F

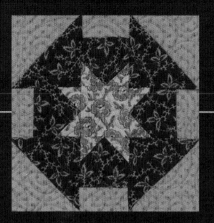

PIE IN THE SKY

Gather your favorite prints and colors and play matchmaker to your heart's content as you blend them into this pleasing patchwork bed quilt. So incredibly simple to sew, yet devastatingly complex in appearance, this quilt is one you'll want to dream under night after night.

Materials

The number of assorted prints used for this quilt can be reduced by purchasing half-yard cuts of 24 assorted prints, and then cutting along the center fold of each half-yard piece to yield two fat quarters, for a total of 48.

48 fat quarters (18" x 22") of assorted prints for blocks, sashing, and border
⅔ yard of dark print for binding
72" x 92" rectangle of batting

Cutting

Cut all pieces across the width of the fabric unless otherwise noted. Please note that for the purpose of cutting, a lengthwise fat-quarter measurement of 22" is assumed. If your lengths differ slightly, don't worry—the strips cut from the fat quarters will easily accommodate all of the pieces needed, even if they aren't quite 22" in length.

From the length of *each* of the 48 fat quarters, cut:

2 strips, 1½" x 22"; crosscut *1* strip into 8 squares, 1½" x 1½" (384 total)

3 strips, 2½" x 22"; crosscut *2* strips into 16 squares, 2½" x 2½" (768 total)

1 strip, 3⅞" x 22"; crosscut into 4 squares, 3⅞" x 3⅞", and then cut each square in half diagonally to yield a total of 8 triangles (384 total)

From the dark print, cut:

8 strips, 2½" x 42" (binding)

Organizing the Patchwork Pieces

Separate the patchwork pieces cut from *each* fat quarter into the following sets, grouping them by print.

Background Sets

1 strip, 1½" x 22"
4 triangles

Churn Dash Sets

1 strip, 2½" x 22"
4 triangles

Star Sets

8 squares, 1½" x 1½"
1 square, 2½" x 2½"

Sashing/Border Sets

15 squares, 2½" x 2½". If you layered your fat quarters for cutting as suggested in the Pin Point tip above right, just group together your layered sets of sashing/border squares; the individual prints can be separated later, if desired, when you stitch your patchwork.

Piecing the Blocks

Sew all pieces with right sides together unless otherwise noted.

1. Select a set of block background pieces cut from one print and a set of Churn Dash pieces cut from a second print. Join the 1½" x 22" and 2½" x 22" strips along one long edge to make a strip set. Press the seam allowance toward the wide Churn Dash strip. Crosscut the strip set into four segments, 2½" wide.

2½"

Make 1 strip set.
Cut 4 segments.

2. Join a background triangle to a Churn Dash triangle, stitching along the long raw edges. Press the seam allowances toward the Churn Dash triangles. Trim away the dog-ear points. Repeat for a total of four half-square-triangle units.

Make 4.

Finished quilt: 66½" x 86½" • Finished blocks: 8" x 8"
Designed by Kim Diehl. Machine pieced by Deb Behrend and Kim Diehl. Machine quilted by Deborah Poole.

3. Select a set of star pieces cut from a third print. Use a pencil to draw a diagonal line on the wrong side of each 1½" square. Layer a prepared square over one corner of a strip-set segment from step 1, placing it on the wide Churn Dash print. Stitch the pair together exactly on the drawn line. Repeat for a total of four pieced units. Referring to "Pressing Triangle Units" on page 10, press and trim the star points. In the same manner, sew, press, and trim the remaining 1½" prepared squares, placing them in mirror-image positions to form four pieced star-point units.

Make 4.

4. Lay out the half-square-triangle units, the 2½" square, and the pieced star-point units as shown to form a block. Join the pieces in each horizontal row. Press the seam allowances of the top and bottom rows toward the outer large triangle units. Press the seam allowances of the middle row toward the center square. Join the rows. Press the seam allowances toward the middle row.

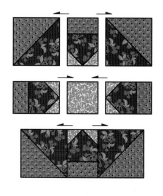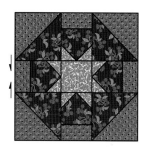

5. Repeat steps 1–4 for a total of 48 blocks measuring 8½" square, including the seam allowances.

PIN POINT

Recycling Your Extra Strip Sets

Rather than waste my leftover strip-set lengths, I cut them into 1½"-wide segments and pieced them together to make scrappy little doll quilts, framing the centers with borders that finished at ¼"- and 2"-wide respectively. These were so simple and quick to make that I had time to add big-stitch hand quilting, and they made perfect gifts for special friends.

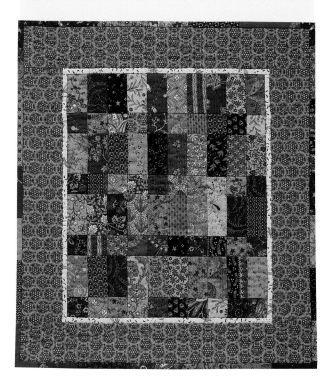

Piecing the Sashing and Border Strips

1. Select 33 assorted print 2½" squares. Join the squares to make a row. Press the seam allowances in one direction. Repeat for a total of 11 rows. To give you added flexibility as you piece your blocks, there are a handful of extra squares.

Make 11 rows.

2. Select two rows from step 1. Reverse the direction of one row to allow the seam allowances to nest together. Join the two rows. Press the center seam allowances to one side. Repeat for a total of two double rows for the top and bottom borders. The remaining rows are for the horizontal sashing.

Make 2 double rows.

3. Select four assorted print 2½" squares. Join the squares to make a strip. Press the seam allowances in one direction. Repeat for a total of 72 vertical sashing strips.

Make 72.

Piecing the Quilt Top

1. Select six blocks and nine vertical sashing strips. Lay out the pieces as shown to make a horizontal block row. Press the seam allowances away from the blocks. Repeat for a total of eight block rows.

Make 8 rows.

2. Referring to the quilt photo, lay out the top and bottom border rows, the block rows, and the horizontal sashing rows to form the quilt top. Join the rows. Press the seam allowances away from the block rows. The pieced quilt top should now measure 66½" x 86½", including the seam allowances.

Completing the Quilt

Refer to "Finishing Techniques" on page 22 for details as needed. Layer the quilt top, batting, and backing. Quilt the layers. The featured quilt was machine quilted in an overall swirling pattern as provided in "Machine Quilting" on page 24 and the border was quilted with diagonal lines through the squares to form a crosshatch. Join the eight dark print 2½" x 42" strips into one length and use it to bind the quilt.

PIE IN THE SKY PILLOWCASE

Finished pillowcase: 20" x 29"

Materials (for one pillowcase)

1⅞ yards of neutral print for pillowcase, patchwork, and lining

5 chubby sixteenths (9" x 11") of assorted prints for patchwork

5 squares, 2½" x 2½", of assorted prints for patchwork

Cutting

From the *lengthwise grain* of the neutral print, cut:

1 rectangle, 20½" x 59½"

From the remainder of the neutral print, cut:

1 rectangle, 7½" x 20½"

20 rectangles, 1½" x 2½"

20 squares, 1½" x 1½"

From *each* of the 5 assorted print chubby sixteenths, cut and organize by print:

2 squares, 2½" x 2½" (10 total)

8 squares, 1½" x 1½" (40 total)

Sewing the Patchwork

1. Choose a matching set of assorted print chubby sixteenth pieces; use a pencil and acrylic ruler to lightly draw a diagonal line on the wrong side of the 1½" squares. Layer a prepared 1½" square over one end of a neutral print 1½" x 2½" rectangle as shown; stitch the pair together on the drawn line. Press and trim as instructed in "Pressing Triangle Units" on page 10. In the same manner, stitch, press, and trim a second prepared 1½" square, placing it in a mirror-image position. Repeat for a total of four pieced rectangles.

Make 4.

2. Join a pieced rectangle to each opposite side of a matching print 2½" square. Press the seam allowances toward the center square. Join a neutral print 1½" square to each end of the remaining pieced rectangles. Press the seam allowances toward the neutral squares. Join these rectangles to the remaining sides of the patchwork unit. Press the seam allowances toward the center square.

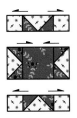

3. Repeat steps 1 and 2 for a total of five star units measuring 4½" square, including the seam allowances. Reserve the remaining 2½" squares.

4. Join the five star units to form a row; press the seam allowances open. Lay out and join the reserved 2½" squares from step 3 and the remaining 2½" squares to form a row; press the seam allowances open. Join these two pieced rows; press the seam allowances toward the row of 2½" squares.

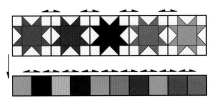

Assembling the Pillowcase

1. Join the neutral print 7½" x 20½" rectangle to the joined-squares side of the patchwork unit. Press the seam allowance toward the patchwork unit. Join the star-row side of the patchwork unit to the neutral print 20½" x 59½" rectangle. Press the seam allowances toward the patchwork unit.

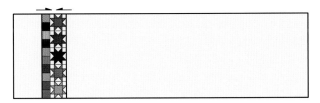

2. Fold under the long raw edge of the neutral print 7½" x 20½" rectangle ¾"; press the crease. Fold under the entire rectangle so that the folded edge extends about ¼" beyond the patchwork; pin in place to form the front lining. (The raw folded edge will be hidden between the layers.) From the front, stitch along both long seams of the star unit row to anchor the lining in place.

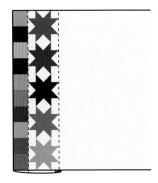

3. Fold under the short raw edge of the neutral print 20½" x 59½" rectangle ½"; press the crease. Fold under this end again 6½"; pin in place to form the back lining and press the newly formed fold. (The folded raw edge should be hidden between the layers.) From the back, stitch through the layers along the first folded edge to anchor the lining.

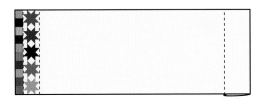

4. With right sides together, fold the pillowcase piece in half, aligning the folded ends. Pin the long side edges together. Stitch the side edges together using a ¼" seam allowance, beginning and ending with a backstitch. Turn the pillowcase right side out and press the side seams flat from the front.

PIE IN THE SKY THROW PILLOW

Finished pillow: 14" x 14"

Materials

3 chubby sixteenths (9" x 11") of assorted prints for center block
1 fat eighth (9" x 22") of dark print for border
4 squares, 3½" x 3½", of coordinating dark print for border corner posts
1 square, 15" x 15", of fabric for pillow back
1 square, 15" x 15", of batting
1 square, 15" x 15", of muslin for pillow-top backing (for machine quilting only)
Fiberfill

Cutting

From 1 assorted print chubby sixteenth for the star, cut:
1 square, 2½" x 2½"
8 squares, 1½" x 1½"

From 1 assorted print chubby sixteenth for the churn dash, cut:
1 rectangle, 2½" x 11"
2 squares, 3⅞" x 3⅞"; cut in half once diagonally to yield 4 triangles

From 1 assorted print chubby sixteenth for the background, cut:
1 strip, 1½" x 11"
2 squares, 3⅞" x 3⅞"; cut in half once diagonally to yield 4 triangles

From the dark print, cut:
4 rectangles, 3½" x 8½"

Piecing the Pillow Front

1. Referring to steps 1–4 of "Piecing the Blocks" on page 52, piece the block for the pillow center.
2. Join dark print 3½" x 8½" rectangles to opposite sides of the block. Press the seam allowances toward the rectangles.
3. Join a coordinating dark print 3½" square to each end of the remaining dark print 3½" x 8½" rectangles. Press the seam allowances toward the rectangles. Join these pieced rectangles to the remaining sides of the block. Press the seam allowances toward the pieced rectangles. The pieced pillow front should measure 14½" square, including the seam allowances.

Completing the Pillow

Refer to "Finishing Techniques" on page 22 for details as needed. If you are hand quilting, layer the pillow front and batting. If you prefer to machine quilt, layer the pillow front, batting, and muslin backing. Quilt the layers. With right sides together, center the quilted pillow front over the back; pin in place. Stitch the layers together using a ¼" seam allowance, leaving a 2" to 3" opening for turning. Clip away the fabric at each sewn corner a few threads outside the seam. Turn the pillow right side out, stuff with fiberfill, and hand stitch the opening closed.

YESTERDAY REMEMBERED

Remember days past when grandma's house
was filled with beautiful linens, softly mellowed
and crisply pressed? Recapture your memories
with this timelessly classic quilt that has
whisper-soft appliqués on a field of green
and a delicate sprinkling of buttons.

Materials

1⅞ yards of olive green print for blocks, appliqués,
    border, and binding
7 fat eighths (9" x 22") of assorted neutral prints
    for blocks and appliqués
1 fat quarter (18" x 22") of neutral striped fabric for
    stems and appliqués
1¼ yards of fabric for backing
42" x 42" square of batting
Bias bar
Water-soluble marker
12 small vintage buttons (optional)

Cutting

Cut all pieces across the width of the fabric in the order given unless otherwise noted. Refer to pages 68 and 69 for appliqué patterns A–G and to "Invisible Machine Appliqué" on page 11 for pattern-piece preparation. Refer to "Cutting Bias Strips" on page 8 to cut bias strips.

From the olive green print, cut:

2 strips, 12½" x 42"; crosscut into 4 squares, 12½" x 12½"

2 strips, 6½" x 24½"

2 strips, 6½" x 36½"

4 strips, 2½" x 42" (binding)

From the *bias* of the remaining olive green print, cut:

1 rectangle, 1" x 15" (this rectangle can be pieced from shorter lengths, if needed)

From *each* of the 7 assorted neutral print fat eighths and the neutral striped fat quarter, cut:

2 squares, 6½" x 6½" (16 total)

Reserve the scraps for the appliqués.

From the *bias* of the remaining neutral striped fabric, cut:

4 rectangles, 1" x 6"

1 rectangle, 1" x 10"

8 rectangles, 1" x 3½"

From the remainder of the assorted neutral print fat eighths and neutral striped fabric, cut a *total* of*:

4 using pattern A

4 pairs of bias rectangles, 1" x 3½", to match the A vase prints

4 using pattern B

12 using pattern C

16 using pattern D

208 using pattern E

4 using pattern F

52 using pattern G

*Piece and trim the patchwork blocks as described in "Piecing and Appliquéing the Blocks" at right first, and then use the remaining neutral print and striped scraps to prepare the above appliqués.

Piecing and Appliquéing the Blocks

Sew all pieces with right sides together unless otherwise noted.

1. Use a pencil and acrylic ruler to lightly draw a diagonal line on the wrong side of each neutral 6½" square.

2. Layer prepared neutral squares over two opposite corners of an olive green print 12½" square. Stitch the pairs together on the drawn lines. Press and trim as instructed in "Pressing Triangle Units" on page 10. Layer an assorted neutral square over each remaining corner of the olive square; stitch, press, and trim as previously instructed. Repeat for a total of four pieced squares measuring 12½" square, including the seam allowances. Use the scraps from the assorted neutral prints, the neutral striped fabric, and the olive green print to cut out the appliqués as described in "Cutting" at left.

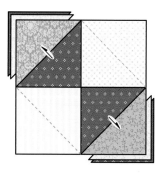

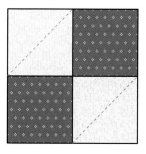

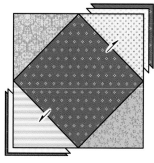

Finished quilt: 36½" x 36½" • **Finished blocks:** 12" x 12"
Designed, machine pieced, and machine appliquéd by Kim Diehl. Machine quilted by Deborah Poole.

3. With right sides together, fold each pieced block in half vertically and lightly press a center crease. Referring to "Making Bias-Tube Stems and Vines" on page 14, prepare each of the neutral 1"-wide bias rectangles. Crosscut the 10" finished stem into eight 1"-long pieces.

4. Referring to the quilt photo, position a prepared vase appliqué onto the right side of the creased block about ⅜" in from the bottom seams of the olive green square; pin in place. Dot the center crease with liquid glue at approximately 1" intervals. Press a 6" stem onto the crease, tucking the bottom raw edge under the vase approximately ¼". Position and pin a prepared B flower over the stem as shown. Referring to "Basting Appliqués" on page 15, use this flower to lay out and baste two 3½" stems in mirror-image positions onto the background (it isn't necessary that these stems extend to the center stem). Position and baste two 1" stems in mirror-image positions above the pinned flower, tucking them well under the center stem and trimming away any edges that may protrude. Last, position and baste two prepared 3½" bias handles (in the print matching the vase) on each upper side of the vase appliqué, tucking the raw ends under the edge approximately ¼". Remove the vase and flower. Referring to "Stitching the Appliqués" on page 15, appliqué the stems and vase handles in place.

5. Reposition, baste, and stitch the vase appliqué. Referring to "Removing Paper Pattern Pieces" on page 17, remove the paper pattern piece. Replace and pin the B flower appliqué, using it to position and baste twelve prepared E leaf appliqués and three prepared C flower appliqués onto the block. Remove the B appliqué; stitch the C and E appliqués in place. Remove the paper pattern pieces.

6. Work from the bottom layer to the top to position, baste, and stitch two prepared D heart appliqués and a G appliqué to the end of each side stem, adding one prepared B flower, one prepared F flower center, and one prepared G appliqué onto the center stem. Remove the paper pattern pieces before adding each new layer.

7. Repeat steps 4–6 for a total of four appliquéd blocks.

Piecing and Appliquéing the Quilt Center

1. Lay out the appliquéd blocks in two rows of two blocks each to make a four-patch unit. Join the blocks in each horizontal row. Carefully press the seam allowances of each row in opposite directions, taking care not to apply heat to the front of the appliqués. Join the rows. Carefully press the seam allowances in one direction.

2. Trace the wreath guide on page 69 onto freezer paper and cut it out. Fold the guide in half vertically, and then horizontally, finger-pressing the creases. With the waxy side down, align the guide creases with the seams of the quilt center; use a hot, dry iron to carefully fuse it in place. Dot the seam of the prepared 15" olive green stem with liquid glue and press it on the background exactly along the guide edge, starting and stopping at a seam; trim away any excess length. Remove the wreath guide and appliqué the stem in place.

3. Use the reserved olive green scraps from step 2 of "Piecing and Appliquéing the Blocks" to prepare 24 leaves using pattern E and 8 berries using pattern G. Using the quilt photo as a guide, position, baste, and stitch the appliqués along the stem. Remove the paper pattern

pieces. The pieced and appliquéd quilt center should measure 24½" square, including the seam allowances.

Appliquéing and Adding the Border

1. With right sides together, fold each olive green border strip in half lengthwise and lightly press the center crease. Refold each strip in half crosswise and press a second center crease. Use a water-soluble marker to place a dot on each border strip where the creases intersect. For the 24½" strips, work out from the center dot at 3" intervals along the lengthwise crease to place three dots on each side, for a total of seven marked dots on each strip. In the same manner, mark each 36½" strip with a total of 11 dots.

Make 2.

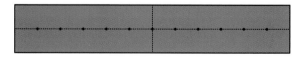

Make 2.

2. Center and baste a prepared G berry over each marked dot on the border strips. Referring to the quilt photo, position and baste four prepared E leaves around each berry. Stitch the appliqués in place; remove the paper pattern pieces.

3. Join 24½" border strips to the right and left sides of the quilt center. Press the seam allowances toward the borders. Join the 36½" border strips to the remaining sides of the quilt center. Press the seam allowances toward the borders.

4. Position, baste, and stitch one prepared G berry and four prepared E leaves over the remaining area of each border corner to complete the design. Remove the paper pattern pieces. The finished quilt top should now measure 36½" square.

Completing the Quilt

Refer to "Finishing Techniques" on page 22 for details as needed. Layer the quilt top, batting, and backing. Quilt the layers. The featured quilt was intricately machine quilted using a variety of designs including feathered hearts, pumpkin seeds, and vines. Cross-hatching, channel quilting, stippling, and curved cross-hatching were used to fill in the areas behind the appliqués and feathers. If desired, hand sew a vintage button to the center of each small appliquéd flower. Join the four olive green print 2½" x 42" strips into one length and use it to bind the quilt.

YESTERDAY REMEMBERED
FRAMED COTTON-AND-WOOL BLOCK

Finished block (excluding frame): 12" x 12"

Materials

1 square, 12½" x 12½", of neutral cotton print for block background

4 squares, 6½" x 6½", of medium cotton print for block corners

2 bias rectangles, 1" x 9", of brown cotton print for stems

1 rectangle, 6" x 8", of black wool for vase appliqué

Assorted wool scraps, including some green, for appliqués

⅛ yard of HeatnBond Lite iron-on adhesive

#8 or #12 perle cotton

Size 5 embroidery needle

14" x 14" square of batting

Bias bar

3 vintage buttons (optional)

Picture frame

Cutting

Refer to pages 68 and 69 for pattern pieces A–G and to "Preparing Wool Appliqués" on page 20 for pattern-piece preparation.

From the 6" x 8" rectangle of black wool, cut:

1 using pattern A

2 bias rectangles, ¼" x 3½"

From the assorted wool scraps, cut a *total* of:

1 *each* using patterns B and F

3 using pattern C

4 using pattern D

12 using pattern E

3 using pattern G

Piecing and Appliquéing the Block

1. Referring to steps 1 and 2 of "Piecing and Appliquéing the Blocks" on page 62, use the neutral print 12½" square and four medium print 6½" squares to piece one block background.

2. Referring to "Making Bias-Tube Stems and Vines" on page 14, prepare the two brown print bias stems. From one prepared stem, cut one 6" length and two 1" lengths; from the second prepared stem, cut two 3½" lengths.

3. Referring to "Turn-Free Hand Appliqué" on page 17 and "Stitching Wool Appliqués" on page 21, follow steps 1–4 to hand appliqué the stems and overhand stitch the wool appliqués. Please note that for this project two ¼" x 3½" bias wool rectangles were used for the vase handles and they were appliquéd with a large hand-sewn decorative zigzag stitch.

Completing the Project

Refer to "Finishing Techniques" on page 22 and to "Big-Stitch Quilting" on page 24 for details as needed. Layer the pieced and appliquéd block with the batting. Quilt the layers. The featured block was quilted in the big-stitch method, with the appliqués outlined to emphasize their shapes. Straight lines were stitched along the inner block seams, radiating outward toward the block corners at ¾" intervals. If desired, hand sew a vintage button to the center of each small flower, and then frame your block.

Patterns do not include seam allowances.

A

B

C

C

If you want to simplify your stitching, use this modified pattern with inner curves rather than points.

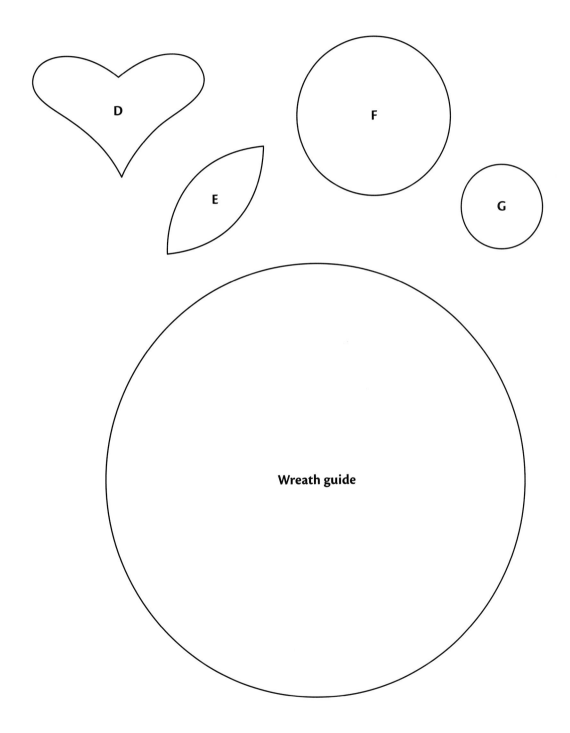

Patterns do not
include seam allowances.

D

E

F

G

Wreath guide

ALL FOWLED UP

Do you continually find yourself in a fowl mood? If so, give in to your yearnings and feather your nest with this simply sewn lap quilt fashioned from richly hued cotton prints and black woolly roosters.

Materials

⅞ yard *each* of 6 assorted prints for blocks and border corner posts

1⅞ yards of black print for border and binding

8 rectangles, 8" x 10", of assorted black wool for appliqués

4¼ yards of fabric for backing

74" x 74" square of batting

1 yard of HeatnBond Lite iron-on adhesive

#8 or #12 perle cotton

Size 5 embroidery needle

Cutting

Cut all cotton pieces across the width of the fabric unless otherwise noted. Refer to page 77 for appliqué patterns A and B and to "Preparing Wool Appliqués" on page 20 for pattern-piece preparation.

From *each* of the 6 assorted prints, cut:
6 strips, 1½" x 42" (36 total)
6 strips, 2½" x 42" (36 total)

From the *lengthwise grain* of the black print, cut:
4 strips, 4½" x 60½"
5 strips, 2½" x 60½" (binding)

From the black wool, cut:
8 using pattern A
8 using pattern B

Piecing the Rail Fence Blocks

Sew all pieces with right sides together unless otherwise noted.

1. To make the small Rail Fence blocks, select one 1½" x 42" strip from each of the six assorted prints. Join the strips along the long edges. Press the seam allowances in one direction. Repeat for a total of six identical strip sets. Crosscut each strip set at 6½" intervals to make 36 blocks measuring 6½" square, including the seam allowances.

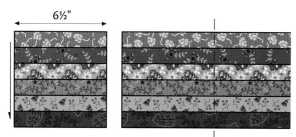

6½"

Make 6 small strip sets.
Cut 36 blocks.

2. To make the large Rail Fence blocks, repeat step 1 to piece six strips sets from the assorted print 2½" x 42" strips and crosscut them at 12½" intervals to make 16 blocks measuring 12½" square, including the seam allowances. From the remainder of the strip sets, cut three segments, 2½" wide; reserve these for use in the border.

Piecing the Quilt Center

1. Referring to the quilt photo, lay out the small Rail Fence blocks in six rows of six blocks, rotating them as shown to form the pattern. Join the blocks in each row. Press the seam allowances toward the blocks with vertical strips. Join the rows. Press the seam allowances open.

2. Lay out three large Rail Fence blocks as shown to form a vertical side row. Join the blocks. Press the seam allowances open. Repeat for a total of two pieced rows. Join these rows to the right and left sides of the quilt center. Press the seam allowances away from the quilt center.

3. Lay out five large Rail Fence blocks as shown to form a horizontal row. Join the blocks. Press the seam allowances open. Repeat for a total of two pieced rows. Join these rows to the remaining sides of the quilt center. Press the seam allowances away from the quilt center.

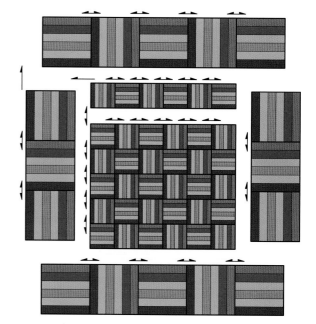

Finished quilt: 68½" x 68½" • Finished blocks: 6" x 6" and 12" x 12"
Designed, machine pieced, and hand appliquéd by Kim Diehl. Machine quilted by Deborah Poole.

Adding the Border

1. Join a black print 4½" x 60½" strip to the right and left sides of the quilt center. Press the seam allowances toward the black print.

2. Using the three reserved 2½" segments from the large Rail Fence strip sets, remove the stitching in any necessary seams to leave eight joined pairs of squares. Join these pairs to make four pieced four-patch units. Press the center seam allowances to one side.

3. Join a four-patch unit to each end of the remaining black print strips. Press the seam allowances toward the black print. Join these pieced strips to the remaining sides of the quilt center. Press the seam allowances toward the black print. The pieced quilt top should now measure 68½" square, including the seam allowances.

PIN POINT

Patchwork Shower Curtains

Simply pieced lap quilts like this one (minus the wool appliqués!) can make striking shower curtains, and they're easy to adapt for this use. For one option, on the back of the quilt, hand sew a 4"-wide hanging sleeve about 2" down from the top edge and slide it onto a shower curtain rod, hanging the rod in front of a second rod pre-hung with a liner. Or, you can hand sew small plastic rings along the top quilt edge directly beneath your binding seam using the number of rings needed to coincide with those hanging your existing shower curtain; use these rings to hook your quilt over the existing curtain.

Appliquéing the Roosters

Referring to the quilt photo, center a prepared B base appliqué onto a Rail Fence block, centering it from right to left and positioning the bottom straight edge flush with the border seam; pin in place. Position a prepared A rooster appliqué onto the block, tucking the bottom raw end under the B appliqué approximately ¼". Baste both appliqués in place as instructed in "Basting Appliqués" on page 15. Referring to "Decorative Stitches" on page 21, overhand stitch the appliqués in place. Repeat for a total of eight appliquéd blocks.

Completing the Quilt

Refer to "Finishing Techniques" on page 22 and "Big-Stitch Quilting" on page 24 for details as needed. Layer the quilt top, backing, and batting. Quilt the layers. The featured quilt was machine quilted with Xs over the connecting strips of the small Rail Fence blocks in the quilt center to form a stair-step pattern; the open areas in between were quilted with serpentine feathers. The large open Rail Fence blocks were quilted with feathered Xs, the background of the appliquéd blocks were echo quilted, and the black border was quilted with a cross-hatching design. Last, big-stitch hand quilting was used to anchor the rooster centers with heart shapes. Join the five black print 2½" x 42" strips into one length and use it to bind the quilt.

PIN POINT

Creating a Stair-Step Pattern

To achieve the stair-step pattern running diagonally across the featured quilt center, choose a dominant hue or print for the Rail Fence blocks and place it in the top or bottom position when assembling your strip sets.

ALL FOWLED UP
EMBELLISHED KITCHEN TOWEL

Finished towel: 20" x 28"

Materials

1 purchased 20" x 28" kitchen towel

1 rectangle, 7" x 10", of black print for rooster appliqué

1 rectangle, 2" x 5", of coordinating black print for rooster base appliqué

1 square, 10" x 10", of HeatnBond Lite iron-on adhesive

Black all-purpose thread

Embellishing the Towel

1. Referring to page 77 for appliqué patterns A and B and to "Fusible Appliqué" on page 18 for preparation and stitching details, prepare one each of the rooster and base appliqués.

2. Thread the sewing machine with black thread. Using a decorative machine stitch, stitch the hem line around the perimeter of the towel; for this project I used a briar design. (You may wish to experiment with a small test piece to practice turning corners and determine how your machine ends the stitch pattern.)

3. Fold the bottom edge of the towel in half and lightly press a center crease; use this crease to position the rooster and base appliqués on the center of the towel about 1½" up from the bottom edge, overlapping the base onto the rooster approximately ¼". Use a satin stitch to appliqué the shapes in place.

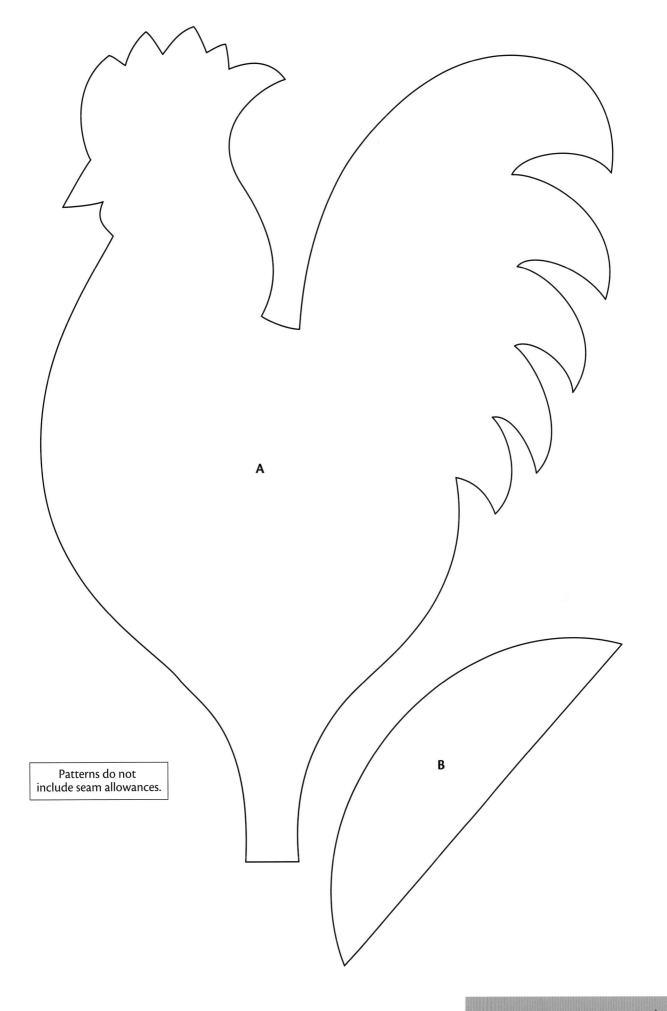

A

B

Patterns do not include seam allowances.

WELCOME WAGON

Extend the warmth of your welcome
to one and all when you stitch this
simple and inviting patchwork lap quilt.
Completely perfect for using those last
little scraps of your favorite prints,
and so quick to sew, you'll find
yourself wanting more than one!

Materials

51 rectangles, 6¼" x 12½", of assorted prints for
    blocks
1½ yards of dark striped fabric or print for outer
    border
½ yard of tan print for inner border
4 yards of fabric for backing
63" x 68" rectangle of batting

Cutting

Cut all strips across the width of the fabric unless otherwise noted.

From the tan print, cut:
4 strips, 1½" x 25½"
4 strips, 1½" x 24"

From the dark striped fabric or print, cut:
2 strips, 5½" x 42½"
2 strips, 5½" x 37½"
7 strips, 2½" x 42"* (binding)

If you are using a striped fabric and want to create a candy-cane effect, cut enough 2½"-wide bias strips to make a 248" length of binding when joined end to end.

Preparing and Piecing the Blocks

Sew all pieces with right sides together unless otherwise noted.

1. Cut each assorted print 6¼" x 12½" rectangle in half to make two squares, 6¼" x 6¼"; this will result in a total of 102 squares. Next, cut each square in half diagonally to make two triangles for a total of 204 triangles.

Cut 102 squares.

Cut 204 triangles.

2. Join two assorted print triangles along the long bias edges. Press the seam allowances to one side. Trim away the dog-ear points. Repeat for a total of 102 half-square-triangle units.

Make 102.

3. Cut each half-square-triangle unit in half diagonally as shown to yield 204 pieced triangles.

Cut 204.

4. Select two pieced triangles sewn from different prints. Repeat step 2 to join the pieced triangles. Repeat for a total of 102 Hourglass blocks measuring 5½" square, including the seam allowances.

Make 102.

PIN POINT

Fanning Seams

To keep the patchwork for this and other pieced projects soft and pliable, you can add a quick step to reduce the bulk of any seam that you feel is overly stiff and heavy. To do this, simply turn your work to the wrong side, remove a few threads from the end of each seam where they intersect, and use your iron on a hot, dry setting to fan them flat into a circle.

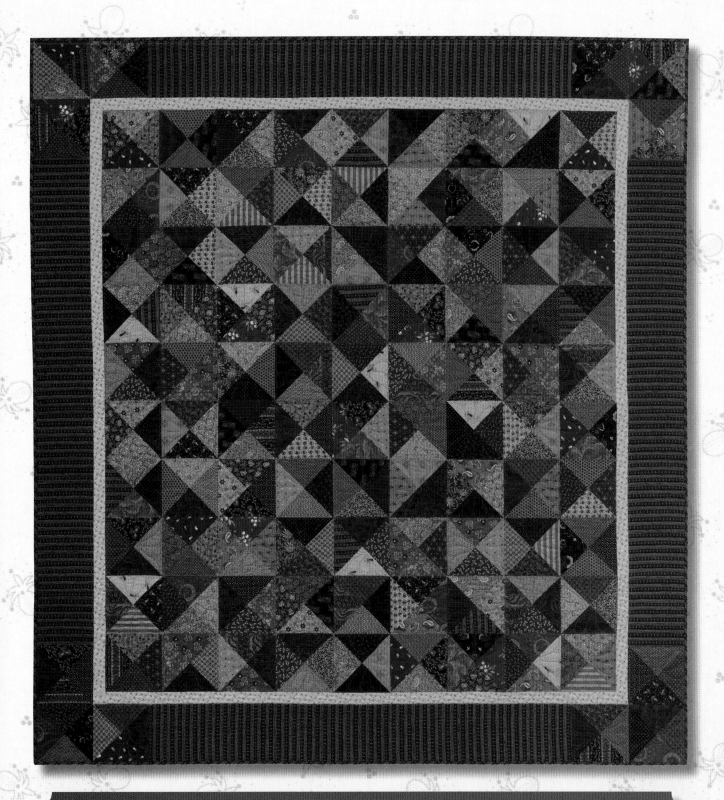

Finished quilt: 57½" x 62½" • Finished blocks: 5" x 5"
Designed by Kim Diehl. Machine pieced by Vicki Jones, Heather Lofstrom, and Jan Watkins.
Machine quilted by Deborah Poole.

Piecing the Quilt Center

Lay out the blocks in 10 rows of nine blocks; reserve the extra blocks for use in the border. Join the blocks in each row. Press the seam allowances of each row in an alternating direction. Join the rows. Press the seam allowances open.

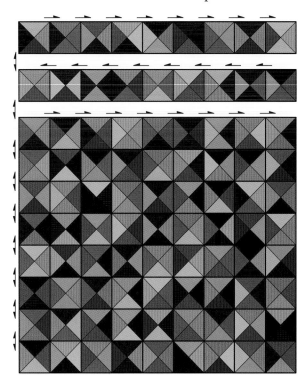

Piecing and Adding the Borders

1. Join two tan print 1½" x 25½" strips; press the seam allowances open. Repeat to make a second pieced strip. Join these pieced strips to the right and left sides of the quilt center. Press the seam allowances toward the tan strips. In the same manner, piece together and join the 1½" x 24" strips to the remaining sides of the quilt center.

2. Join one reserved Hourglass block to each end of the two dark 5½" x 42½" strips. Press the seam allowances toward the dark print. Join these pieced strips to the right and left sides of the quilt top.

3. Join two reserved Hourglass blocks to each end of the two dark 5½" x 37½" strips. Press the seam allowances toward the dark strips. Join these pieced strips to the remaining sides of the quilt top. The pieced quilt top should now measure 57½" x 62½".

Completing the Quilt

Refer to "Finishing Techniques" on page 22 for details as needed. Layer the quilt top, batting, and backing. Quilt the layers. Each block of the featured quilt was machine quilted with a square feathered wreath radiating out from a cinnamon-roll swirl center. Xs were stitched onto the tan inner border to form a cross-hatching pattern and the stripes of the outer-border print were outlined. Join the seven dark print 2½"-wide strips into one length and use it to bind the quilt.

WELCOME WAGON YO-YO QUILT

Finished quilt: 52½" x 52½"
Finished blocks: 5" x 5"
Designed by Kim Diehl. Machine pieced and appliquéd by Vicki Jones, Heather Lofstrom, and Jan Watkins. Machine quilted by Deborah Poole.

Materials

36 fat eighths (9" x 22") or equivalent scraps of assorted prints for yo-yos
⅝ yard *each* of 6 assorted neutral prints for blocks
1⅛ yards of red print for outer border and binding
½ yard of cream striped fabric or print for inner border
12 squares, 6¼" x 6¼", of assorted prints for border blocks
3½ yards of fabric for backing
#8 or #12 perle cotton
Size 5 embroidery needle

Cutting

Refer to page 89 for the large and small yo-yo patterns.

From *each* of the 6 assorted neutral prints, cut:
14 squares, 6¼" x 6¼" (84 total); cut each square in half diagonally to yield 2 triangles (168 total)

From the cream striped fabric or print, cut:
4 strips, 1½" x 20½"
4 strips, 1½" x 21½"

From the red print, cut:
4 strips, 5½" x 32½"
6 strips, 2½" x 42" (binding)

From the assorted print fat eighths, cut a *total* of:
64 using the large yo-yo pattern
524 using the small yo-yo pattern

Piecing the Hourglass Blocks

Sew all pieces with right sides together unless otherwise noted.

1. Using the neutral print triangles, follow steps 2–4 of "Preparing and Piecing the Blocks" on page 80 to piece 64 Hourglass blocks for the quilt center. To give you added flexibility as you piece your blocks, there are a handful of extra triangles.

2. Cut the assorted print 6¼" squares in half once diagonally to make 24 triangles. Repeat step 1 to make 12 Hourglass blocks for the border.

Making the Yo-Yos

Select a large yo-yo fabric circle. With the wrong side up, turn a portion of the edge toward you a scant ¼" to create a hem. Using a knotted length of perle cotton and the embroidery needle, bring the needle up through the hem from the wrong side of the folded fabric to bury the knot between the layers. Sew a running stitch through all of the layers, near the folded edge. Continue turning the hem to the front and stitching as you work your way around the circle to your starting point; gently pull the threaded needle to gather the yo-yo edges into the center. Insert the needle under the gathered edge, just to the side of the center opening, and bring it out on the back of the yo-yo. Knot and clip the thread from the back, keeping the gathers taut. Repeat for a total of 64 large yo-yos. In the same manner, stitch 524 yo-yos using the small yo-yo fabric circles.

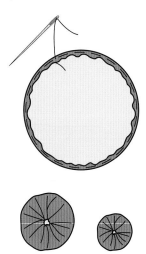

Make 64.   Make 524.

Appliquéing the Yo-Yos

1. Position a large yo-yo over the intersecting center seams of a neutral Hourglass block. Referring to "Basting Appliqués" on page 15, baste the yo-yo in place. Position and baste a small yo-yo over each diagonal seam immediately next to the center yo-yo, and then complete the circle with four additional yo-yos. Use your favorite appliqué method to stitch the yo-yos in place. Repeat for a total of 64 yo-yo–embellished blocks.

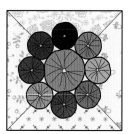

Make 64.

2. Position, baste, and stitch one small yo-yo onto the center of each assorted print Hourglass block.

Assembling the Quilt Center

1. Lay out the neutral appliquéd blocks in eight rows of eight blocks. Join the blocks in each row. Press the seam allowances open. Join the rows. Press the seam allowances open.
2. Referring to step 1 of "Piecing and Adding the Borders" on page 82, use the cream 1½" x 20½" strips to add the inner borders to the left and right sides and the cream 1½" x 21½" strips to add the inner borders to the remaining sides.
3. Referring to steps 2 and 3 of "Piecing and Adding the Borders" on page 82, use the embellished Hourglass blocks and the red print 5½" x 32½" strips to finish the quilt. The pieced quilt top should measure 52½" square, including the seam allowances.

Completing the Quilt

Refer to "Finishing Techniques" on page 22 for details as needed. Layer the quilt top, batting, and backing. Quilt the layers. For the featured quilt, the background of each horizontal row was alternately machine quilted with feathered petals or free-form repeating lines. A rope design was quilted onto the inner border, with a double cross-hatching pattern stitched onto the red borders. Last, a square feathered wreath was quilted around each yo-yo in the border corner blocks. Join the six red print 2½" x 42" strips into one length and use it to bind the quilt.

PIN POINT

Creating a Thread Guide

For sewing machines without an upright spool position, it's easy to create your own thread guide to stabilize your monofilament. Use a piece of masking tape over the clasp end of a closed safety pin and attach it to the back side of the sewing machine, placing it behind your spool pin position so that the curved "elbow" end sits slightly above the top machine surface. Place the spool of monofilament on the table behind your sewing machine, feed the monofilament through the looped elbow of the safety pin, and continue threading as usual.

WELCOME WAGON QUILTED DOOR HANGER

Finished project: 4" x 12"
(excluding hanger and tassel)

Materials

4 squares, 5¼" x 5¼", of assorted neutral prints

1 square, 8" x 8", of green print for stem and leaf appliqués

10 squares, 4½" x 4½" and smaller, of assorted prints for yo-yos

1 square, 3½" x 3½", of black print for vase appliqué

1 rectangle, 5" x 13", *each* of backing and batting

2 yards of black baby rickrack (¼"-wide)

1 purchased black 2" tassel (optional)

Fiberfill

#12 perle cotton in black and neutral colors

Size 5 embroidery needle

Water-soluble marker

Cellophane tape

Cutting

Refer to page 89 for the large and small yo-yo patterns and appliqué patterns A and B and to "Invisible Machine Appliqué" on page 11 for pattern-piece preparation.

From the black print, cut:
1 using pattern A

From the green print, cut:
1 rectangle, 1" x 6½"
4 using pattern B

From the squares of assorted prints, cut:
1 using the large yo-yo pattern
9 using the small yo-yo pattern

From the rickrack, cut:
8 pieces, 9" long

Piecing and Appliquéing the Door Hanger

1. Referring to steps 1–4 of "Preparing and Piecing the Blocks" on page 80, use the assorted neutral print 5¼" squares to piece three Hourglass blocks measuring 4½" square, including the seam allowances. Discard the remaining pieced triangles. Join the blocks end to end to make a 4½" x 12½" background unit. Press the seam allowances in one direction.

2. Fold the bottom block of the background unit in half vertically through the center seams and press the crease; in the same manner, press a horizontal crease. Use a pencil and an acrylic ruler to lightly draw a line from each creased side edge to the bottom creased edge, forming a V shape. (The background will be trimmed along these lines later.)

3. Center the prepared A vase onto the bottom background square with the top edge about ¼" below the horizontal block seam; pin in place.

4. Referring to "Making Bias-Tube Stems and Vines" on page 14 and "Basting Appliqués" on page 15, prepare the green 1" x 6½" stem and press it onto the center of the background, tucking the bottom raw edge under the vase approximately ¼". Referring to "Stitching the Appliqués" on page 15, stitch the stem and vase in place.

5. Stitch the yo-yos as instructed in "Making the Yo-Yos" on page 84. Referring to the project photo, use the large yo-yo to position the small yo-yos into a flower design, overlapping them randomly as necessary to make them fit. Apply a dot or two of liquid glue under each small yo-yo to anchor them in place. Remove the large yo-yo and appliqué the small yo-yos.

6. Reposition and baste the large yo-yo. Next, lay out and baste four B leaf appliqués and the remaining small yo-yo. Appliqué all pieces to the background; remove the paper pattern pieces as instructed in "Removing Paper Pattern Pieces" on page 17.

Completing the Door Hanger

Refer to "Finishing Techniques" on page 22, "Big-Stitch Quilting" on page 24, and "Stem Stitch" on page 21 for details as needed.

1. Use a water-soluble marker and a light box or window to transfer the "Welcome" design to the top edge of the hanger, taking care not to position it within the top ¼" seam allowance.

2. Layer the door hanger top and batting. Quilt the layers. The featured project was quilted in the big-stitch method along the seam line; the appliqués and yo-yos were outline quilted and a vein runs through the center of each leaf. Use black perle cotton to stem stitch the "Welcome" design, sewing through the batting layer to prevent shadowing.

3. Trim the bottom of the hanger along the drawn lines and trim the remaining batting flush with the background edges.

4. Slightly fan the 9" rickrack ends into a cluster and, with the ends flush, use tape to anchor them to the top of the background about ½" in from the side edge as shown. Twist the rickrack cluster once and anchor the remaining ends to the opposite top edge. Stay stitch the rickrack in place through the tape, about ⅛" down from the top edge. Pin the loop of rickrack to the background to anchor it away from the edges; remove the tape. Stay stitch the hanging end of the tassel to the bottom point of the background; use tape or a pin to anchor it to the center.

5. With right sides together, center the hanger over the backing fabric; pin the edges in place. Use a ¼" seam allowance to stitch the hanger to the backing, beginning along one side and leaving a 2" to 3" opening for turning. Trim away the excess backing fabric and turn the hanger right side out. Lightly stuff with fiberfill and hand stitch the opening.

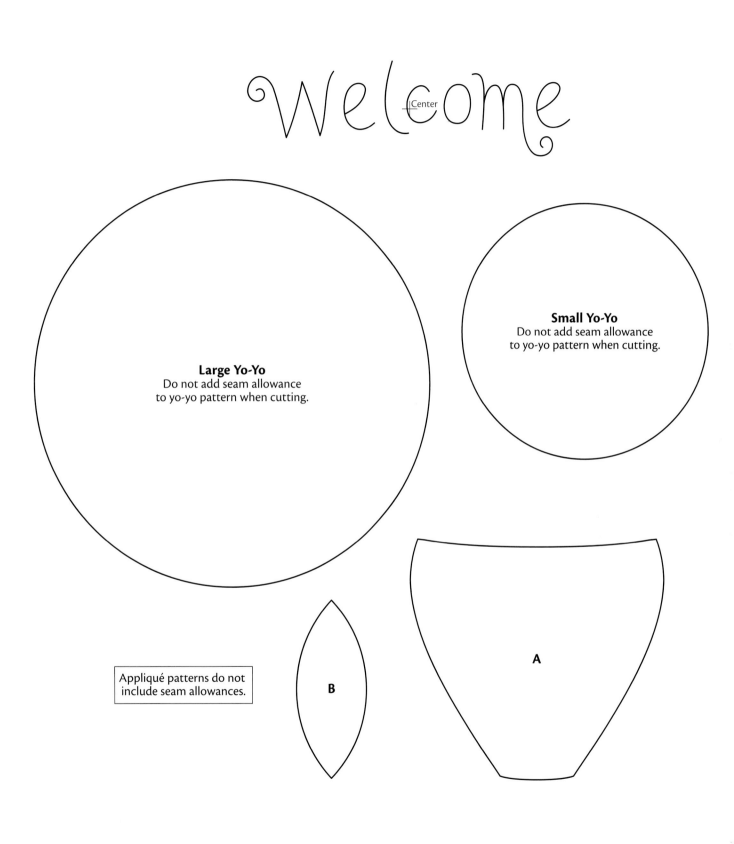

Welcome

Center

Large Yo-Yo
Do not add seam allowance
to yo-yo pattern when cutting.

Small Yo-Yo
Do not add seam allowance
to yo-yo pattern when cutting.

Appliqué patterns do not
include seam allowances.

B

A

FRONT PORCH POSIES

Awash with memories of gently swaying rocking chairs, freshly squeezed lemonade, and pots of trailing flowers on the porch, this lavishly appliquéd quilt brings to mind carefree summer days with sun-warmed fabric posies that will bloom for many seasons to come.

Materials

16 fat quarters of assorted prints (including some red) for middle border Churn Dash blocks, flower appliqués, and berry appliqués

3 yards of muted gold print for background

1 fat quarter (18" x 22") of cranberry print for center churn dash unit and berry appliqués

1⅛ yards of medium green print for vines, leaf appliqués, and binding

½ yard of light green print for leaf and small flower appliqués

1 fat quarter of coordinating green print for oak leaf appliqués

1 fat eighth (9" x 22") of black print for large flower center appliqués

4 yards of fabric for backing

72" x 72" square of batting

Bias bar

Water-soluble marker

Cutting

Cut all pieces across the width of the fabric unless otherwise noted. Refer to "Cutting Bias Strips" on page 8 to cut bias strips. For greater ease in preparation, cutting instructions for the appliqués are provided separately.

From the muted gold print, cut:

2 strips, 11" x 42". From *1* strip, cut a 20½" length; cut this piece in half lengthwise to make 2 strips, 5½" x 20½". From the remainder of this strip, cut 2 squares, 8⅞" x 8⅞"; cut each square in half diagonally *once* to yield a total of 4 triangles. From the second strip, cut one 30½" length; cut this piece in half lengthwise to make 2 strips, 5½" x 30½". From the remainder of the strip, cut 4 squares, 4½" x 4½".

From the *lengthwise grain* of the remaining muted gold print, cut:

2 strips, 8½" x 50½"

2 strips, 8½" x 66½"

From the remainder of the muted gold print, cut:

1 square, 4½" x 4½"

From the cranberry print, cut:

2 squares, 8⅞" x 8⅞"; cut each square in half diagonally *once* to yield a total of 4 triangles

4 squares, 4½" x 4½"

Reserve the scraps for the appliqués.

From *each* of the 16 assorted print fat quarters, cut:

4 squares, 4⅞" x 4⅞"; cut each square in half diagonally *once* to yield a total of 8 triangles (128 total)

9 squares, 2½" x 2½" (144 total)

Reserve the scraps for the appliqués.

From the medium green print, cut:

7 strips, 2½" x 42"

From the *bias* of the remaining medium green print, cut:

2 rectangles, 1¼" x 7"

12 rectangles, 1¼" x 9"

16 rectangles, 1¼" x 4"

8 rectangles, 1¼" x 12"

16 rectangles, 1¼" x 13"

4 rectangles, 1¼" x 7½"

Reserve the scraps for the appliqués.

Preparing the Appliqués

Refer to page 99 for appliqué patterns A–E and to "Invisible Machine Appliqué" on page 11 for pattern-piece preparation. Prepare the following appliqués:

24 using pattern A (flower) from assorted print fat-quarter scraps

25 using pattern B (large flower center) from black print

25 using pattern C (small flower center) from light green print

112 using pattern C (berry) from cranberry print and assorted red fat-quarter scraps

10 and 10 reversed using pattern D (oak leaf) from coordinating green print fat quarter

104 and 104 reversed using pattern E (leaf) from light green and medium green print scraps

Appliquéing and Piecing the Center Block

Sew all pieces with right sides together unless otherwise noted.

1. Referring to "Preparing Bias-Tube Stems and Vines" on page 14, prepare the assorted length medium green 1¼"-wide strips.

2. Referring to "Basting Appliqués" on page 15, baste two prepared 7" stems diagonally onto a gold 4½" square, positioning them to form an X shape. Referring to "Invisible Machine Appliqué" on page 11, appliqué the stems in place. From the back, use scissors to trim away the excess stem length, leaving the ends flush with the block corners.

Finished quilt: 66½" x 66½" • **Finished center block:** 30" x 30" • **Finished Churn Dash border blocks:** 10" x 10"
Designed, machine pieced, and machine appliquéd by Kim Diehl. Machine quilted by Celeste Freiberg.

3. Fold a prepared B appliqué in half horizontally and vertically and finger-press the creases. Align the appliqué creases with the 7" stems on the step 1 square to perfectly center the shape; baste and stitch in place. Referring to "Removing Paper Pattern Pieces" on page 17, remove the paper pattern pieces. In the same manner, position, baste, and stitch a C appliqué to the center of the B appliqué; remove the paper pattern piece.

4. Layer a cranberry print and gold print 8⅞" triangle; fold the layered triangles in half at the long bias edge and finger-press a center crease. Join the pair along this edge, leaving an approximately 2" opening at the crease for adding the vine. Press the seam allowance toward the cranberry print. Trim away the dog-ear points. Repeat for a total of four half-square triangle units.

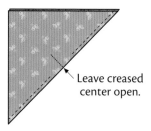

Leave creased center open.

Make 4.

5. Join a 4½" cranberry square to a 4½" gold print square. Press the seam allowances toward the cranberry print. Repeat for a total of four pieced rectangles.

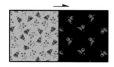

Make 4.

6. Lay out four half-square-triangle units, four pieced rectangles, and the appliquéd 4½" square to form a Churn Dash unit. Join the pieces in each horizontal row. Press the seam allowances toward the rectangle units. Join the rows. Press the seam allowances toward the middle row, finger-pressing the stems to help direct the center-square seams if needed.

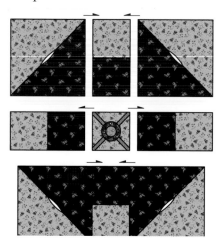

7. Join a gold print 5½" x 20½" strip to opposite sides of the Churn Dash unit. Press the seam allowances toward the gold strips. Join a gold print 5½" x 30½" strip to each remaining side of the Churn Dash unit. Press the seam allowances toward the gold strips. The pieced center block should measure 30½" square, including the seam allowances.

8. With right sides together, fold and press the block to form two diagonal creases, one center vertical crease, and one center horizontal crease. Measure 3" out from the sashing seam at each of the vertical and horizontal creases and use a water-soluble marker to mark a small dot.

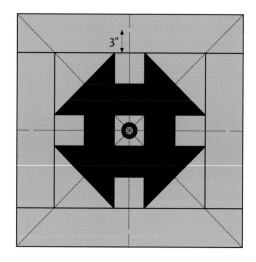

9. Referring to the quilt photo, glue baste a 9" stem and press it onto a diagonal corner crease, tucking the raw end into the seam opening approximately ¼". In the same manner, lay out two 4" stems on each side of the 9" stem, placing them in mirror-image positions and tucking the raw ends under the center stem. Next, position a 12" stem on each side of the 9" stem, tucking the raw ends into the seam opening and curving them outward toward the marked dots (it isn't necessary that the 12" stems meet the marked dots). Repeat with the remaining block corners. Stitch the stems in place.

10. Work from the bottom layer to the top to position, baste, and stitch one A, B, and C appliqué to the top of each corner stem and each marked dot, remembering to remove the paper pattern piece before adding each new layer. In the same manner, refer to the quilt photo to position, baste, and stitch seven E appliqués, seven E reversed appliqués, one D appliqué, one D reversed appliqué, and eight C berry appliqués onto each corner of the block.

11. Position, baste, and stitch four D appliqués to the center square of the block, and one C berry appliqué between each pair of E leaves. Remove the paper pattern pieces.

Piecing the Middle Border

1. To make a Churn Dash block, select four triangles and four squares cut from the same fat-quarter print for the Churn Dash foreground pieces and four triangles and five squares cut from a different fat-quarter print for the Churn Dash background. Follow steps 4–6 of "Appliquéing and Piecing the Center Block" on page 94 to sew the block, disregarding the instructions for leaving an opening in the seams for the vines. Repeat for a total of 16 Churn Dash blocks measuring 10½" square, including the seam allowances.

2. Join three blocks end to end. Press the seam allowances in one direction. Repeat for a total of two pieced border strips. Join these strips to the right and left sides of the center block. Press the seam allowances toward the center block, taking care not to apply direct heat to the appliqués.

3. Repeat step 2 to make two additional pieced strips, using five blocks for each strip. Join these strips to the remaining sides of the center block. Press the seam allowances toward the center block.

PIN POINT

Artfully Displaying Your Quilts

Creating a focal point for displaying your wall- or lap-sized quilts is easy to do. Simply choose a complementary or neutral shade of paint and apply it to the wall where you wish to display your quilt, covering a section to echo the shape of your quilt and extending it to be about 4" to 6" larger on all sides. Frame the edge of the painted area with finished molding strips, and hang your quilt in the center for an instant "wow" factor.

Adding and Appliquéing the Outer Border

1. Join gold print 8½" x 50½" strips to the right and left sides of the quilt top, leaving a 2" opening at the outer edge of both seams of the center Churn Dash block for adding the vines; in addition, leave the outermost ends (about 2") of the border strip seams unsewn for adding the vines. Do not press the seams of these strips at this time. Fold the outer edge of the right border strip in half and finger-press a center crease. Measure in 2¼" from this creased edge to mark a small dot as previously instructed. Using the seam line joining the two outermost Churn Dash blocks as a guide, measure in 2¼" from the long raw edge at each end of the border strip and mark a small dot. Repeat with the left side of the quilt top.

2. For the right border strip, refer to the quilt photo to baste and position a 9" stem at each seam opening along the center Churn Dash block, ensuring each raw end is tucked into the seam approximately ¼" and curving it out toward the marked center dot. Next, position and baste a 13" vine onto each open end of the strip, curving it out toward the outer marked dots. Stitch the vines in place. Use all-purpose thread and your sewing machine to stitch the seam openings. Carefully press the seam allowances toward the border strip. Repeat with the left border strip.

3. Referring to the quilt photo, position, baste, and stitch three A, B, and C appliqués to each border strip as previously instructed. Add 18 E appliqués, 18 E reversed appliqués, and 15 C berry appliqués, positioning them along the vines.

4. Referring to step 1, join one gold print 8½" x 66½" strip to each remaining side of the quilt top, leaving openings in the seams at the outermost edge of each corner Churn Dash

block to add the vines. Mark three small dots on the strips as previously instructed.

5. Position, baste, and stitch the stems and vines as instructed in step 2 and stitch the seam openings.

6. Referring to step 3, work from the bottom layer to the top to stitch the remaining A through D appliqués to the border strips.

7. Turn under one raw end of each 7½" stem approximately ¼" and anchor it in place with fabric glue stick. Fold each border corner in half diagonally and lightly press a center crease extending from the outer edge down to the middle border seam.

8. Position and baste a prepared 7½" stem onto each border corner, aligning the turned end onto the corner of the Churn Dash block between the previously appliquéd stems. Position and baste a 4" stem on each side of the center stems in mirror-image positions, ensuring the raw ends are tucked well under the center stem. Stitch the stems in place.

9. For each border corner, work from the bottom layer to the top to stitch the remaining A through E appliqués as previously instructed.

Completing the Quilt

Refer to "Finishing Techniques" on page 22 for details as needed. Layer the quilt top, batting, and backing. Quilt the layers. The featured quilt was machine quilted with a repeating design of curved lines on the center Churn Dash block, with a small stipple design stitched in the background. A serpentine feathered cable was quilted over the middle border Churn Dash blocks. For the outer border, teardrop shapes were quilted along the vines to echo the shape of the E leaves and a small stipple design was used to fill in the remaining background areas. Join the seven medium green print 2½" x 42" strips into one length and use it to bind the quilt.

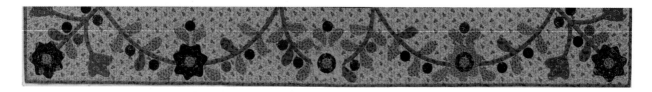

FRONT PORCH POSIES
WOOL SUNGLASSES SLEEVE

Finished sleeve: 3½" x 7"

Materials

1 square, 7½" x 7½", of wool for outer sleeve
1 square, 7½" x 7½", of coordinating cotton print
    for lining
Assorted wool scraps for appliqués
1 bias strip, ¼" x 5½", of green wool for stem
1 square, 5" x 5", of HeatnBond Lite iron-on
    adhesive
#8 or #12 perle cotton
Size 5 embroidery needle
1 small button (optional)

Cutting

Refer to page 99 for appliqué patterns A, B, C, and
E, and to "Preparing Wool Appliqués" on page 20
for pattern-piece preparation. It isn't necessary to
cut away the centers of the shapes cut from iron-on
adhesive.

From the assorted wool scraps, cut a *total* of:
1 *each* using patterns A and B
4 using pattern C
2 using pattern E
1 using pattern E reversed

Making the Sun Glasses Sleeve

1. Fold the 7½" square of wool in half and lay it flat with the fold positioned on the left. Referring to "Fusible Appliqué" on page 18 and "Basting Appliqués" on page 15, prepare and lay out the appliqué pieces, taking care to allow approximately ¾" between the appliqués and the raw wool edges.

2. Overhand stitch (see page 21) the appliqués and stem to the wool background. If desired, hand sew a button to the flower center.

3. With right sides together, layer the unfolded square of appliquéd wool with the cotton lining; pin the edges. Beginning on the bottom left-hand edge, use a ¼" seam to machine stitch the wool to the lining; leave a 2" opening for turning. Clip away each corner a couple of threads out from the seam line. Turn the sleeve right side out, press the edges, and hand sew the opening closed.

4. Slide an embroidery needle containing knotted perle cotton through the layers at the bottom folded edge, bringing it out at the inner fold. Blanket stitch (see page 21) the front and back edges together working from right to left, sliding the needle underneath the back lining layer for each stitch so they are only visible from the front. When you arrive at the top-right corner, take two stitches in place to anchor it well, and then continue around the top of the case from front to back to embellish the edges, but leaving them open. To end your blanket stitch, take two stitches in place at the back upper-left corner. Knot the thread near the fabric. Insert the needle between the wool and lining layers; tug gently until the knot disappears and clip the thread.

PIN POINT

Multitasking

In addition to protecting your sunglasses, this wool sleeve makes a charming case for your rotary cutter, especially when toting it to classes!

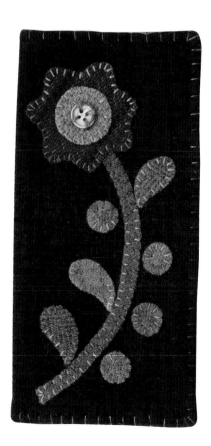

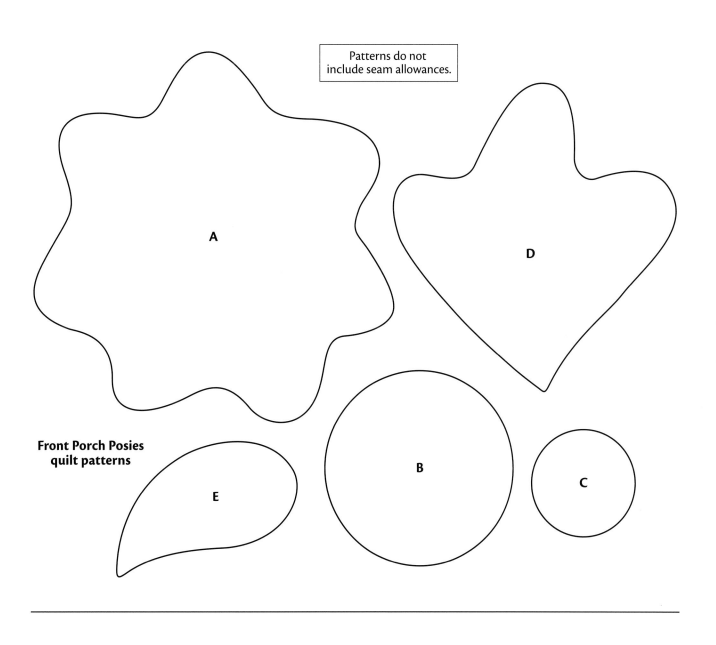

Patterns do not
include seam allowances.

A

D

**Front Porch Posies
quilt patterns**

E

B

C

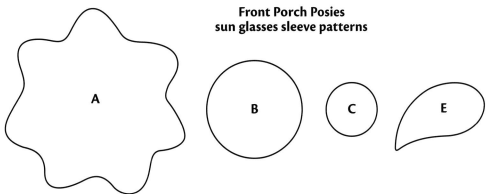

**Front Porch Posies
sun glasses sleeve patterns**

A

B

C

E

PETAL PUSHER

For a perfect fit every time, slip into something comfortable and wrap yourself within the folds of this comfy quilt. Rows of Dresden blossoms adorned with lush leaves and berries will never go out of fashion, and you'll find yourself reaching for this throw again and again.

Materials

68 squares, 7" x 7", of assorted prints for Dresden appliqués

1¾ yards of blue print for border and Dresden appliqué centers

4 fat quarters (18" x 22") of assorted tan prints for blocks

2 fat quarters of assorted cream prints for blocks

½ yard *each* of two assorted cream prints for blocks

½ yard of green striped fabric for leaf appliqués

½ yard of coordinating green print for vines and leaf appliqués

3 chubby sixteenths (9" x 11") of assorted dark cranberry prints for berry appliqués

Enough 2½"-wide random lengths of assorted prints to make a 252" length of binding when joined end to end

3½ yards of fabric for backing

62" x 70" rectangle of batting

Spray starch (Best Press works well and smells pretty!)

Bias bar

Cutting

Cut all pieces across the width of the fabric unless otherwise noted. Refer to page 109 for appliqué patterns A–D and to "Invisible Machine Appliqué" on page 11 for pattern-piece preparation. Refer to "Cutting Bias Strips" on page 8 to cut bias strips. For greater ease in preparation, cutting instructions for the Dresden wedge pieces and appliqués are provided separately.

From the 4 assorted cream prints, cut a *total* of:
18 squares, 8½" x 8½"

From the four assorted tan prints, cut a *total* of:
16 squares, 8½" x 8½"

From the *lengthwise grain* of the blue print, cut:
2 strips, 8½" x 48½"
2 strips, 8½" x 40½"

From the remainder of the blue print, cut:
34 using pattern B

From the *bias* of the coordinating green print, cut:
25 rectangles, 1¼" x 9"

From the remainder of the coordinating green print, cut:
25 using pattern C

From the green striped fabric, cut:
75 using pattern C

From the assorted dark cranberry prints, cut a *total* of:
75 using pattern D

Preparing the Dresden Wedges and Appliqués

Sew all pieces with right sides together unless otherwise noted.

1. Fold each assorted print 7" square in half; use a hot, dry iron to press the crease, forming two layers of fabric. Layer these pressed prints into stacks, with four prints per stack for a total of eight layers.

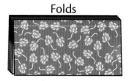

Folds

2. Using the pattern on page 109, trace 34 wedge pieces onto freezer paper and cut them out.

3. Referring to the illustration, use a hot, dry iron to fuse two wedge pieces onto the top layer of each fabric stack from step 1; pin the layers between the paper pieces to stabilize them. Use a rotary cutter and mat to cut out the fabrics exactly along the paper edges for a total of 272 wedges; remove the paper pieces.

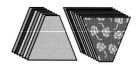

Cut 272 wedges.

4. With right sides together, join the assorted print wedges in pairs, stitching along the long edges and using a ¼" seam allowance. Press the seam allowances open from the wrong side. Next, in the same manner, join and press the pairs to make 68 halves. Last, join and press the halves to make 34 Dresden units. From the front, lightly spray each unit with starch and press it flat.

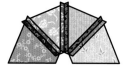

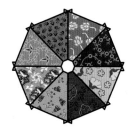

Make 34.

5. Cut 34 freezer-paper pattern pieces using pattern A on page 109. Fold each pattern piece as shown on page 104 and finger-press the creases. Referring to "Preparing Appliqués" on page 12, use a small amount of fabric glue stick to anchor each pattern piece to the wrong side of a Dresden unit, aligning the creases with the seams to perfectly center it. Lay each unit on a

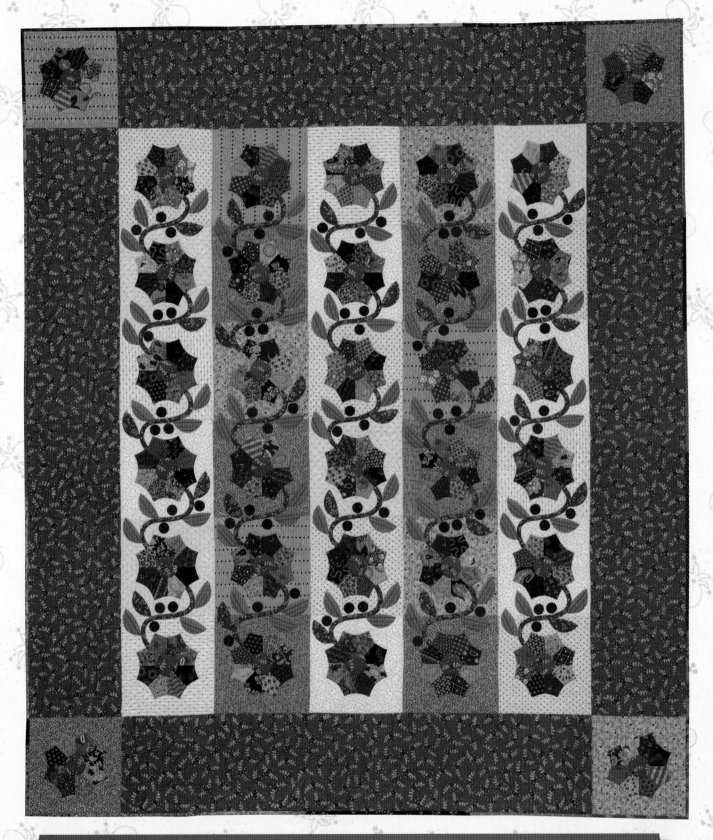

Finished quilt: 56½" x 64½" • **Finished blocks:** 8" x 8"
Designed, machine pieced, and machine appliquéd by Kim Diehl. Machine quilted by Deborah Poole.

cutting mat, pattern side up, and use a rotary cutter to cut out each appliqué, adding a ¼" seam allowance around the paper. For finished appliqué edges, complete the preparation steps provided in "Preparing Appliqués."

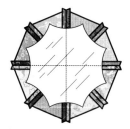

6. Fold each assorted cream and tan print 8½" square in half and lightly press a vertical crease; refold the squares in the opposite direction to press a horizontal crease.

7. Select a prepared 8½" square and a prepared Dresden blossom. Align the seams of the Dresden blossom with the background creases. Referring to "Basting Appliqués" on page 15, baste the appliqué in place, leaving two opposite edges un-basted as shown. Repeat with the remaining 8½" squares and Dresden blossoms. Referring to "Stitching the Appliqués" on page 15, appliqué the blossoms, leaving the un-basted edges open for adding the vines. Do not remove the paper pattern pieces at this time.

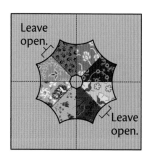

Leave open.

Leave open.

Assembling the Quilt Center

1. Lay out six appliquéd cream squares to form a vertical row, taking care to ensure that the blossom openings are at approximately the ten o'clock and four o'clock positions. Join the squares. Carefully press the seam allowances toward the top of the row. Repeat for a total of three cream rows. In the same manner, lay out, stitch, and press two tan rows, pressing

the seam allowances toward the bottom of the rows. Reserve the four remaining tan blocks for use in the border.

2. Referring to "Making Bias-Tube Stems and Vines" on page 14, prepare the 9" stems.

3. Select a pieced row from step 1. Using the quilt photo as a guide and referring to "Basting Appliqués" on page 15, press a prepared 9" vine onto the background between each Dresden blossom, tucking the raw ends under the blossoms at least ¼" (any extra length will be trimmed away when the paper pattern pieces are removed). If the stems don't curve easily, briefly bring a hot iron down onto them after they've been positioned to relax and smooth the fibers. Lay out and baste one print leaf, three striped leaves, and three berries along each stem. Stitch the appliqués in place. Appliqué the openings left for the stems on each block, including the reserved blocks. Referring to "Removing Paper Pattern Pieces" on page 17, remove the paper pattern pieces. Repeat with the remaining pieced rows.

4. Fold each prepared B circle appliqué in half horizontally and vertically and finger-press the creases. Align these creases with the Dresden blossom seams to position and baste the B appliqués in place; repeat with the reserved blocks. Stitch the B appliqués in place and remove the paper pattern pieces.

5. Referring to the quilt photo, lay out the cream and tan rows in alternating positions. Join the rows. Carefully press the seam allowances toward the tan rows. The pieced quilt center should measure 40½" x 48½", including the seam allowances.

Adding the Borders

Join a blue print 8½" x 48½" strip to the right and left sides of the quilt center. Press the seam allowances toward the blue print. Join a reserved tan appliquéd square to each end of the blue print 8½" x 40½" strips. Press the seam allowances toward the blue print. Join these pieced strips to the remaining sides of the quilt center. The pieced and appliquéd quilt top should now measure 56½" x 64½", including the seam allowances.

Completing the Quilt

Refer to "Finishing Techniques" on page 22 for details as needed. Layer the quilt top, batting, and backing. Quilt the layers. The row backgrounds of the featured quilt were machine quilted alternately with patterns of feathered petals and McTavishing (free-form shapes that are echo quilted inward). The Dresden appliqués were stitched with connecting loops to form teardrop shapes in each wedge and a large-scale feathered spray was quilted onto each blue border strip. Join the random lengths of assorted prints into one length and use it to bind the quilt.

PIN POINT

Rickrack Stems

For appliqué quilts featuring stems and vines, try substituting rickrack for a more whimsical look. After positioning a rickrack stem, baste it to the background using tiny dots of liquid basting glue along the underside at about 1" intervals, and then heat set the glue from the back using a hot, dry iron. For invisible stitches, sew your stems in place along the center of the rickrack using a small zigzag stitch and monofilament thread in the needle, or use regular sewing thread in a matching or complementary color for an additional design element.

PETAL PUSHER COTTON PINCUSHION

Finished size: approximately 4¼" in diameter

Materials

8 squares, 3½" x 3½", of assorted prints for
   Dresden wedges
1 square, 2½" x 2½", of coordinating print for
   center
1 square, 6" x 6", of fabric for pincushion bottom
#8 or #12 perle cotton
Size 5 embroidery needle
Fiberfill
Crushed walnut shells (optional)

Stitching the Pincushion

1. Using the wedge pattern on page 109, trace one piece onto a square of freezer paper. Stack the assorted print 3½" squares together and use a hot, dry iron to fuse the freezer-paper wedge piece to the top fabric. Pin the layers near the paper. Use a rotary cutter and mat to cut out the wedge shapes.

2. Referring to step 4 of "Preparing the Dresden Wedges and Appliqués" on page 102, prepare one Dresden unit.

3. Use freezer paper to trace and cut one each of pattern pieces A and B provided on page 109. Referring to "Preparing Appliqués" on page 12, prepare the B appliqué, and then anchor the A pattern piece to the wrong side of the Dresden unit, aligning the creases with the seams to perfectly center it. With right sides together, layer the Dresden unit with the 6" print square; place this unit paper side up on a mat and use a rotary cutter to cut out the shape, adding a ¼" seam allowance around the paper. Separate the layers.

4. Referring to "Stitching the Appliqués" on page 15, appliqué the B circle onto the center of the Dresden unit. Remove the paper pattern piece using the opening on the back. Stay stitch one curve of the Dresden unit to stabilize the sewn seam, about ⅛" from the edge.

5. With right sides together, reposition and layer the Dresden unit and bottom piece, aligning the points, and pin together. Beginning and ending with a backstitch, use a ¼" seam allowance to join the pieces, leaving approximately a 1½" opening at the stay-stitched edge for turning. Cut away the fabric outside each point, two or three threads away from the seam. Turn the pincushion right side out, firmly stuff with fiberfill, and hand stitch the opening. (For my pincushion, I used crushed walnut shells in the bottom for added weight, and then finished with fiberfill.)

6. Use the perle cotton and embroidery needle to blanket stitch (see page 21) around the center B circle; bury the knotted ends of the thread within the pincushion.

7. Using a 40" length of knotted perle cotton, slide the embroidery needle through the pincushion

to bury the knot and bring it up at the number 1 position along a seam. Pass the needle under the cushion, bringing it up on the opposite side and centering the thread over the seam. Insert the needle where the seam meets the center circle at position 3, sliding it through the fiberfill and bringing it up at the position 4 seam. Pull the thread taut and cross it under the cushion as before, bringing it up on the opposite side once again.

8. Insert the needle at the top of the seam next to the center circle, sliding it through the layers and out at the next seam as previously instructed. Pass the needle under the cushion again, sliding it under the crossed perle cotton strands to catch the threads and bringing it back up to the adjacent seam on the *same* side of the cushion. Insert the needle at the top of the seam where it meets the center and pass it under the circle to exit at the top of the opposite seam. Pull the needle until the thread is taut. Repeat the step of passing the needle under the cushion to catch the threads, inserting it back at the top of the final seam, and then bringing it up and exiting at the top of the adjacent seam. Take two backstitches over the blanket stitch to hide them, knot the thread, and bury it within the cushion. Clip the thread tail.

PETAL PUSHER WOOL PINCUSHION

Finished size: approximately 5⅝" in diameter

Materials

8 squares, 3½" x 3½", of assorted wool for Dresden wedges

1 square, 2½" x 2½", of coordinating wool for center

2 squares, 7" x 7", of wool for pincushion top and bottom

2 squares, 7" x 7", of muslin for lining

#8 or #12 perle cotton

Size 5 embroidery needle

Crushed walnut shells

Funnel

Stitching the Pincushion

1. Use the wedge pattern provided on page 109 to trace eight pieces onto freezer paper; cut out the shapes on the drawn lines. Use a hot, dry iron to fuse a freezer-paper wedge piece onto each 3½" wool square. Use a rotary cutter and mat to cut out the wedges exactly along the paper edges; remove the paper.

2. Referring to step 4 of "Preparing the Dresden Wedges and Appliqués" on page 102, prepare one Dresden unit.

3. Referring to "Fusible Appliqué" on page 18 and the photo, use the A and B patterns on page 109 to prepare the Dresden unit and center circle.

4. Layer the 7" wool and muslin squares; pin the four layers together. Trace the pincushion pattern on page 109 onto freezer paper and fuse it onto the top of the 7" fabric squares. Cut out the shape exactly along the circle edge.

5. Referring to "Basting Appliqués" on page 15, center the prepared B circle onto the Dresden unit and use perle cotton and an embroidery needle to overhand stitch (see page 21) the circle in place. Center and baste the Dresden unit onto a wool circle; use an overhand stitch to appliqué the unit in place. As a decorative element, use perle cotton to stitch Xs over the Dresden wedge seams, placing them randomly.

6. With right sides together, layer the appliquéd wool circle with the second wool circle. Pin the edges and use a ¼" seam allowance and a slightly reduced stitch length to join the edges, leaving an approximate 2¼" opening for turning. In the same manner, join the two muslin pincushion circles. Turn both sets of sewn circles right side out.

7. Insert the muslin liner into the wool pincushion, with the openings aligned. Use a funnel to fill the muslin liner with crushed walnut shells. Hand stitch the muslin opening, and then stitch the wool opening. Blanket stitch (see page 21) around the perimeter of the pincushion. Knot the thread and bury it within the pincushion. Clip the thread tail.

PIN POINT

Pincushion Grippers

Are you tired of chasing your pincushions around the table as you're trying to use them? Here's a quick and simple remedy that will make your pincushion stay put. Cut a small square or circle from a non-skid rug gripper and hand stitch it to the bottom of your pincushion. The gripper will be hidden from view, and your pincushion will remain exactly where you place it!

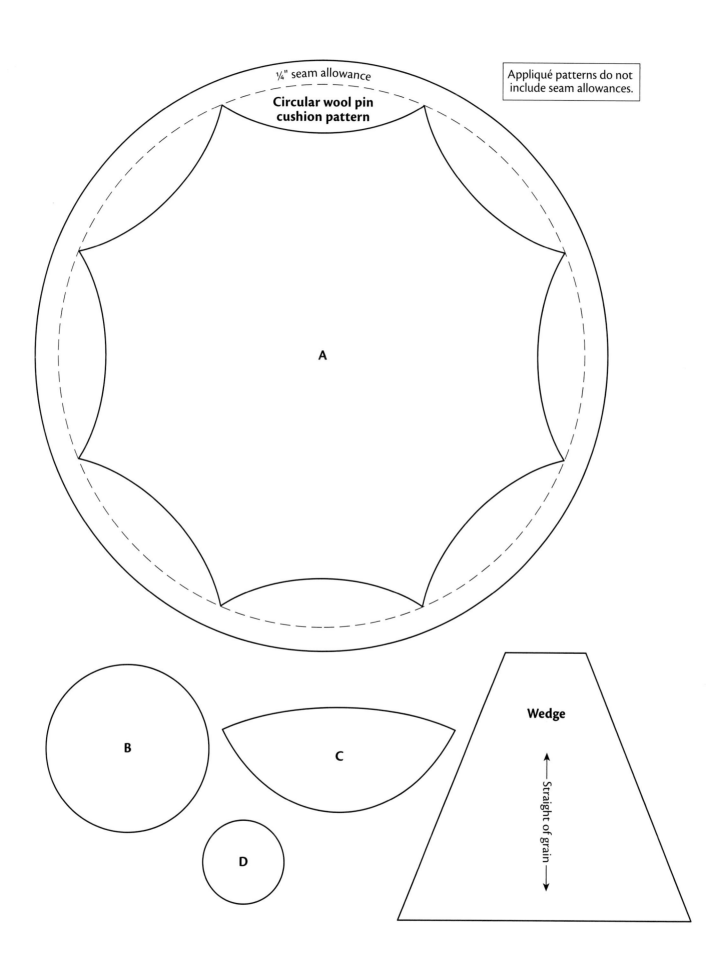

¼" seam allowance

Circular wool pin cushion pattern

Appliqué patterns do not include seam allowances.

A

B

C

D

Wedge

Straight of grain

ABOUT THE AUTHOR

After teaching herself to quilt without the benefit of a mentor or any formal instruction, Kim Diehl entered and won a nationally sponsored quilting challenge in the late 1990s with just the third quilt she'd ever made. With her fourth quilt, Kim began publishing her original designs in *American Patchwork & Quilting* magazine, and has since seen her work featured in numerous national and international publications, including *Australian Homespun* and *Australian Quilter's Companion* magazines.

In 2004, Kim began partnering with Martingale & Company to write her series of "Simple" quilting books, with *Simple Graces* appearing as the fifth title in this best-selling collection.

Even without formal artistic training, Kim was given the opportunity in 2008 to further draw upon her creative instincts, and she has enjoyed designing several fabric collections for Henry Glass in the "scrap-basket" style she loves so much.

When she's not writing books and designing quilts and fabric, Kim travels extensively around the country teaching her invisible machine-appliqué method and sharing her quilts.

THERE'S MORE ONLINE!

For a schedule of Kim's workshops and lectures and information on her books and fabric, visit www.kimdiehl.com. For more great books on quilting, go to www.martingale-pub.com.

You might enjoy these other fine titles from MARTINGALE & COMPANY

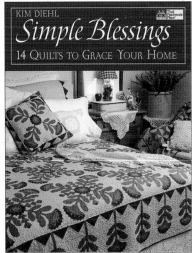

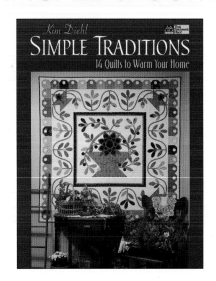

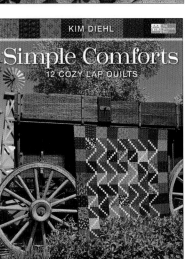

Simple Seasons
Recipe Cards and Tin

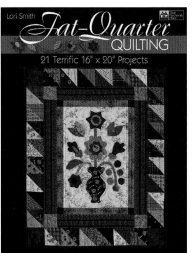

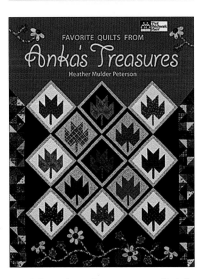

Our books are available at bookstores and your favorite craft, fabric, and yarn retailers.
Visit us at www.martingale-pub.com or contact us at:

1-800-426-3126
International: 1-425-483-3313
Fax: 1-425-486-7596
Email: Info@martingale-pub.com

Martingale®
& C O M P A N Y
America's Best-Loved Craft & Hobby Books®
America's Best-Loved Knitting Books®

That Patchwork Place®
America's Best-Loved Quiting Books®

For Helen

First American Edition 1987   Printed in Hong Kong by South China Printing Co.   10 9 8 7 6 5 4 3 2 1   ISBN 0-02-775640-8

THE
RUNAWAY CHICK

Robin Ravilious

Macmillan Publishing Company   New York

Spry's mother knew she was in for trouble the moment Spry hatched out. He started asking questions as he broke through his shell.

"Hello, Mother! Isn't it bright out here! What makes it all so shiny? Can I go and look?"

"Bless me, NO!" scolded his mother. "Come here at once, and keep safe and warm like your sisters."

She tucked all five chicks into her feathers, and told them how dangerous the big world was.

But Spry watched the mayflies dancing in the sunlight, and paid no attention to warnings. He wanted to go and explore.

Soon he was racing round the farmyard, into mischief from dawn until dusk. He nearly drove his mother to distraction.

He chased bees to see if they were good to eat. He tried to swim like the ducks.

He got stuck in wire fencing,

trod on by a goose,

and very nearly gobbled
by a pig!

He led his sisters into trouble too — inventing naughty games for them to play. They bombed the hens as they dozed in the dustbath.

They made fun of their father behind his back.

They stole all the tastiest creepy crawlies in the compost heap, and guzzled them all themselves.

And they all ran away

and hid, whenever

their poor mother called.

"That chick will come to a bad end," grumbled the older hens. "He's got no more sense than a thistledown seed, and he's too cheeky by half!"

They were very nearly right!

One morning when Mother called, Spry found a new hiding place: in a basket on the farmhouse steps. In he slipped, and burrowed among the vegetables and flowers, giggling wickedly. Next moment — help! — the basket was picked up, and Spry was on his way to who knew where.

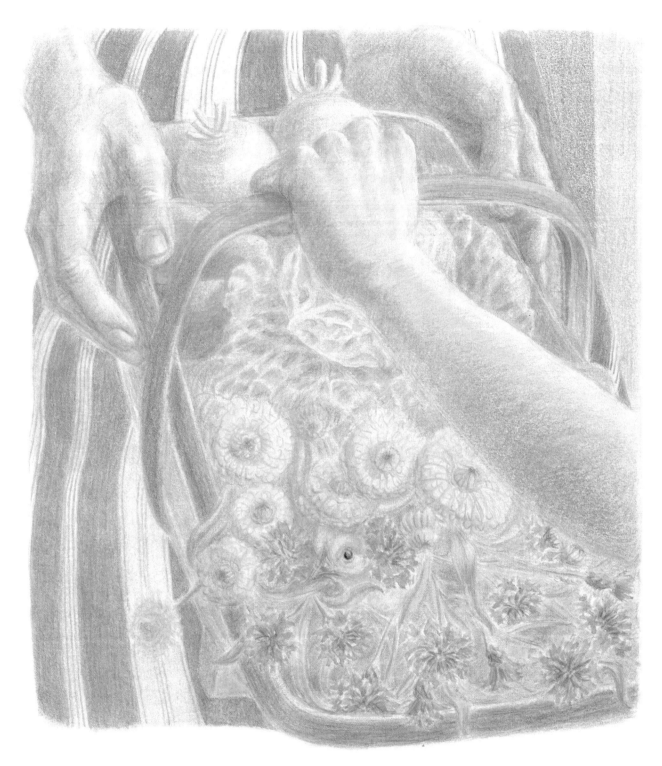

For a long, long time he crouched in the swaying flowers, his little heart frantically ticking. Then there came the sound of knocking, and human voices, and the basket landed with a thump.

The voices went away and all was quiet. Spry peeped out, stared round, and set off to explore. He found himself in a strange, dark place, full of surprising things. . . .

Some were fun. Some were puzzling.

One gave him a nasty fright.

He thought he had better go home.

The window was open. He could see sunlight outside. But... the way was blocked by a large mound of tawny fur! He went to investigate.

Suddenly the mound woke up.

"Aha!" it said. "Breakfast!"

"You can't eat *me*!" squeaked Spry indignantly. "I belong to the farm. Besides, my father would peck you to bits!"

"You don't belong *here*," sneered the cat. "And Daddy's on his dunghill far away."

Spry turned and ran for his life. Now hide-and-seek was not a game anymore. Round and round the room he pattered, hiding here,

hiding there,

. . . but the cat pad-padded after him.

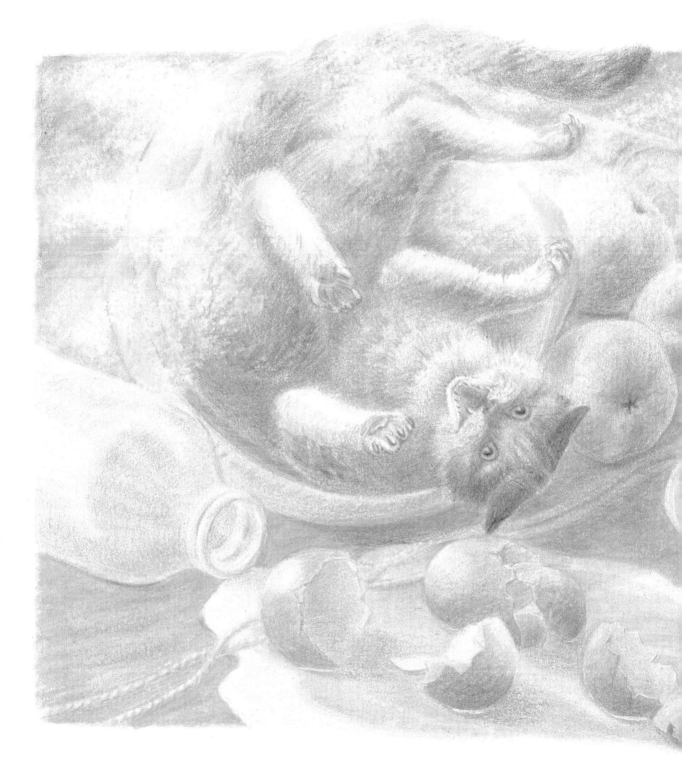

He hid on the table among the cooking things. But the cat kept coming. He dived into some knitting. But the cat was getting ready to spring. With wool caught round one foot, Spry pelted hither and thither, winding a zigzag of yellow yarn.

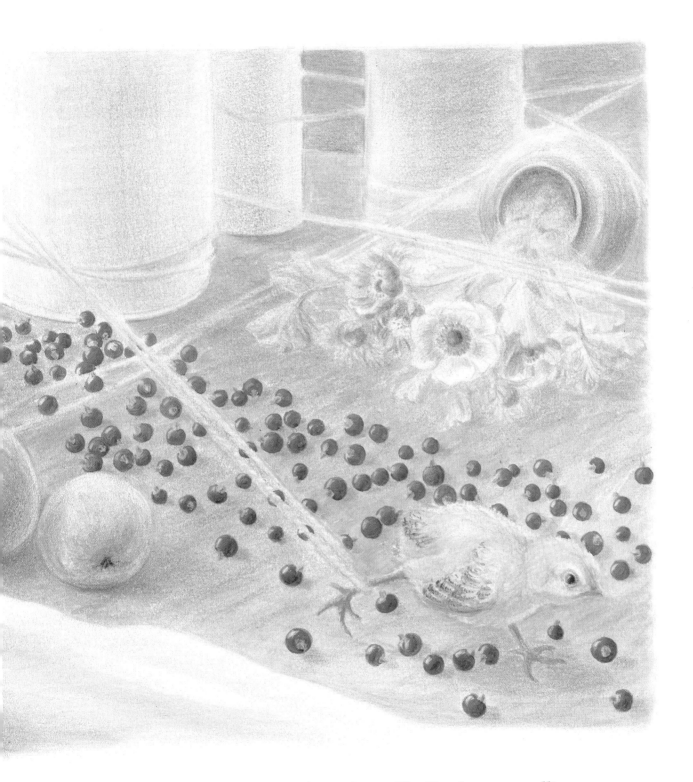

A flower vase tipped over, then the milk. Fruit went rolling, eggs smashed, tins crashed to the floor. Then up sprang the cat. It skidded on the eggs, tripped in the wool, thumped into the mixing bowl, and vanished, yowling, into a snowstorm of flour.

"PUSSY!" yelled an angry voice. "You bad, BAD cat!"
    But the cat was gone, leaping guiltily out of the window like a puff of dirty white smoke.

That left Spry, sticky, bedraggled, and quite worn out, alone in the middle of the mess.

"What on earth . . . ?" exclaimed the voice. "You poor little scrap! However did you get here?"

Gentle hands picked him up. They cleaned, dried, and warmed him, and fed him delicious crumbs.

After all that, it was a very different chick who set out for home, riding perkily in those same kind hands, and looking down on the world as if it all belonged to him.

On the way they passed the cat — still trying to lick all the flour
and egg from its fur.

"Enjoyed your breakfast?" asked cheeky Spry.

The cat turned its back and sulked.

Soon Spry was home and telling everyone his adventures.

"I flew through the sky," he boasted. "And bumped into a fox, and fought off a ferocious great cat!"

No one believed a word. And his father said he would peck him if he ever ran away again.

Later, Spry climbed wearily up to bed in his favorite place, on his mother's pillowy back.

"Good-night, Mother," he murmured sleepily. "Sorry I was bad . . . I *did* see a fox, though — *truly* I did."

"Not another cheep out of *you*!" said his mother, shuddering.

But Spry was already fast asleep.